# CLIMBING THE CHELSEA HILL

## A STORY ABOUT FOOTBALL

CLIMBING THE

# CHELSEA HILL

**A STORY ABOUT FOOTBALL**

THE BIOGRAPHY OF THE ALL-TIME CHELSEA GREAT

# KEN SHELLITO

IN CONVERSATION WITH NICK ATKINSON

Previously published by MPH Group Publishing
This updated edition published by Pitch Publishing, 2020

Pitch Publishing
A2 Yeoman Gate
Yeoman Way
Worthing
Sussex
BN13 3QZ
www.pitchpublishing.co.uk
info@pitchpublishing.co.uk

ISBN 978 1 78531 680 7

Typesetting and origination by Pitch Publishing
Printed and bound in India by Replika Press Pvt. Ltd.

# CONTENTS

# PREFACE

IT WAS in 2009 that I first met Ken and it was over a pint of Kilkenny. A young lad had come over and asked for his autograph. Ken sat him down and chatted for a bit, signed his autograph and the boy was on his way with a big smile and 'I got it, Dad' on his lips. That really summed up the man that I got to know: he always had time for anyone and was always sincere, always a true gentleman.

I was even prouder when he asked me to write his biography and became one of the few people in his life who had access to the whole story. From his humble upbringing in war-torn East London to his own personal paradise here in Sabah. I saw what made him tick, what made him happy, and what made him sad.

He told me of his regrets, his achievements and, most of all, his love for his family here in Sabah.

He credits much of who he was to those early years in East London where everyone came together to help and how his life in Sabah with his family and friends brought back so many of those wonderful memories.

I don't remember this great man having a bad word to say and I will always cherish the times we spent together and to being a part of his life. He was gentle, honest, special, and I am very grateful to him for allowing me to play a small part in his legacy.

Never to be forgotten, Ken. Thank you for being my good friend.

Thank you again to the wonderful fans who have helped me out with pictures, memories and the like. Ken always said that you were the heart of the club and with the support I have received, I fully understand. Cheers to you all.

Nick Atkinson
May 2019

# FOREWORD I

MANY TIMES, in my life of playing football, I've been lucky in that life, lucky to be able to play for such a wonderful club with the most marvellous fans, and lucky to work with and learn from some of the greatest footballers of my era.

One of these great footballers was my friend Ken Shellito. It was a real pleasure for me to join Chelsea, which had already started to train and coach youngsters who had just left school. I was one of these lucky kids. Chelsea had already started to produce some very good young players, and it was paying off, with young players not only playing for Chelsea, but for England as well. We all felt extremely privileged for the life we enjoyed.

Ken was already at the club when we joined, and he made it really easy for us country boys to settle in London.

He was a Londoner, and he went out of his way to help us get settled in. Ken was a bit older than us, he was already doing well, he was a full-back and he stood out with any team he played for at the club. He stood out as a top-class full-back.

He was years before his time in how he played in the position of right full-back. He was very hard to get by, good in the tackle and his use of the ball was as good as any full-back in the league.

His future looked so good leading up to the 1966 World Cup. He would have played in that, but luck was to play a cruel trick on Ken at the start of the '63 season. His place in the Chelsea team was already assured because of his class and style. He had already played for England's first team and life was looking very good until, during an early game at the start of the season, he got injured. His studs caught in the grass as he turned, he was down straight away, and his knee was damaged badly. He was to miss the season.

All of us were shocked and shaken but the good spirit Ken had about himself made him want to fight to get back fit. Being injured when everyone else was playing was hard to take, but Ken kept up the fight without any luck. That knee was to keep Ken out of our side for another two years and for sure he was to miss the World Cup.

However, the quality of the man showed through. Did he give up? No, he went on the coaching staff to help new young lads make a good start. He loved teaching new things and skills and helping. Down that line he was to help Chelsea again by becoming manager. You could not find anyone who loved the club more and he would serve the club to his very best.

Everybody who had the pleasure to play in the same team loved him for his skill, attitude and his love for Chelsea.

Anyone who served under him or was coached by him would speak only of what a good and kind person he was.

Over the past years we have kept in touch by phone. It was always fun to hear his voice, a man I shall be proud to say was my friend. He will be so missed by his family and his many friends and by the thousands of Chelsea fans. I will miss him.

Rest in peace, Ken, my lovely friend.

**Bobby Tambling, ex-Chelsea and England striker**

# FOREWORD II

I MET Ken when I joined the AFC back in 2008 and it was almost immediate that we became the best of friends. He was always a good laugh and gave me invaluable advice throughout, particularly on the coaching side of things. Yes, he was old enough to be my dad, but he was like a brother to me and to be honest, you would never find a guy like him in football today. I remember him talking about this 'crazy world of football with lots of money, lots of ego ... and lots of trouble!' To me, Ken was the last 'knight in shining armour' in the gruesome old world of football.

I learnt so much as a player and a coach from him and he definitely had the best eye for talent I have ever known.

He always told me that the best football is simple football and one of the important lessons I got was how to deal with the senior management at the clubs.

Ken also recommended and put me forward to become the head coach at the Sabah Football Club. I didn't get the job as the management gave it to a local lad and Ken told them straight out they had made the wrong choice and it was a mistake. I went to Kelantan shortly after and we achieved the treble a year later, which is an impressive feat in Malaysia. Sabah were relegated!

Ken was humble to the end; a very proud man and an absolute gentleman and I am very honoured to have been able to share some of his extraordinary life with him. He said football is such an amazing game that no matter who or what you are, on the pitch you are all equal. He told me, 'We can sit and talk for hours about football, you know, and we can be right, and we can be wrong, but that is football.'

Thank you, Ken.

**Bojan Hodak**
**Head Coach, U-19 Malaysian National Team**

# FOREWORD III

I FIRST met Ken Shellito in 1994 in Kuala Lumpur and of course it was on a football pitch. An agent had organised for me to trial in Malaysia and I rocked up to Cheras stadium looking for Ken. I found him, told him who I was and the position I played, upon which Ken told me he was after a foreign centre-back, not a striker. He kindly allowed me to play the game anyway and I scored two goals.

After the game, Ken walked over, shook my hand and said 'Well played.' Unfortunately, he didn't need a striker.

His final words were, 'I know not signing you will come back to haunt me.' Three months later, my new team Sabah beat Ken's Kuala Lumpur 3-1 in the FA Cup semi-final at Merdeka Stadium and I scored. Ken found me after the game and shook my hand. He said, 'You're haunting me,' then smiled and walked away.

Five years later, Ken became the Sabah coach and moved to Kota Kinabalu and it was during this time that our friendship developed. A few years later and by the time Ken had married Jeany and moved to what he affectionately called 'Chelsea Hill' our friendship had developed into a close bond.

Ken Shellito was a real football man. It was in his blood; he knew nothing else. Many a time we sat at Chelsea Hill discussing football, sometimes Malaysian football, sometimes his beloved Chelsea, but never the commercial bits. Ken loved football for the game itself, not for the business side of it.

He played for Chelsea and managed it in a bygone era when you were paid a decent wage and grateful for it. The idea of millionaire players was wrong to him and I loved him for that. The stories from his times at Chelsea were priceless for me. Stories about Jimmy Greaves, Terry Venables or Ray Wilkins, to name a few, were always riveting. If I was to summarise the man Ken Shellito in a few words, I would say, 'Combined his love of football with honesty, loyalty, knowledge, integrity and success and did it on his own terms.'

The last time I saw Ken was in hospital three days before he passed. He was weak and not able to talk much.

We asked him what was Chelsea's biggest ever win and he opened his eyes and whispered, '13-0.' I, of course, went straight to Google and sure enough, Chelsea's biggest-ever win was 13-0 vs Jeunesse Hautcharage from Luxembourg in the UEFA Cup Winners' Cup.

That summed up the man perfectly. Chelsea was forever in his blood.

Goodbye, Ken, I will miss you. RIP.

**Scott Ollerenshaw**
**Tournament Director Malaysia Borneo Football Cup**

# FOREWORD IV

KEN AND I first met at primary school when we were five years old. We played in all the school teams, football, cricket, but not boxing. Ken never took to boxing because he could not bear the pain. Yet this was the boy who would jump up and head the wet, heavy football from goal kicks and corners without flinching.

When we left school, we had some great times with our mates, particularly George, Dave and Bob. This generally involved much drinking and girls. One night, coming home from the Hinds Head in a taxi, we ended up buying it – Ken and I, as we were the only ones who had any money left. Dave was the only one who could drive, so he became the chauffeur. I painted the Chelsea badges on the front doors of the taxi and we used to ferry Ken's mum and dad to Stamford Bridge to the games. We managed to get 11 people in that taxi on many occasions, sounds crazy now.

Ken always managed to get tickets for his mates and George and I used to go to see the internationals with Scotland. We always had a bunch of tickets to sell to pay for the trip. We would not dare charge more than face value to the Scottish lads who used to run down the platform at the St Enoch Station.

Then we all started to get married. Ken was the first in 1964, but we still got together and over the years kept in touch. I live in New Zealand and Ken in Malaysia, but we still managed to have a reunion in England and Ken brought his wife Jeany and we met up in Maldon, Essex where Dave lives. Great times and I wouldn't have missed them for anything.

**Harry Woods, Lifelong Friend**

# INTRODUCTION

IT MAKES me smile when I hear people saying that I was unlucky. 'You got a bad injury at 23 that destroyed your chances for a World Cup winners' medal' is what they say.

I don't see it that way because I am still in professional football after 60 years and to me the basis of that is from my upbringing. Two characteristics that I have are determination and companionship, which I gained from an early age in the East End of London. And I seriously think that if you've got those two things in life, especially in the world of football, then you have a fair chance of having a good life.

That is just what I have had, a good life; I have done a lot, seen a lot and am now excited that the chance to share this with you has arrived.

The determination to succeed came from being in a low-income bracket – a very low-income bracket. This did not make me financially hungry but, more importantly, it made me want to achieve something.

As you read on I trust you will appreciate what made me tick, what now makes me tick and realise that I am proud of my background, my upbringing and my life and achievements in football. The companionship comes from being born during the Second World War and growing up in an environment that could only succeed with people working, living and believing together.

It is with pleasure that I am telling my story, in my words and in my own way. Like it or not, there will be things you may disagree with but it is a tale of a life that was fun and a life that was rewarding. Not for the money, not for the medals, but for the people I shared it with and the great friends I still have. From the start, they have been a part of my life as I made my way through the highs and lows, the ups and downs and the proud moments that have littered my career.

The beautiful game of football has been a dominant force in my life for more than 62 years and I will never tire of it. I trust you will be entertained by how the game was played at the start of my career and how it has changed in today's environment of the high-profile glitz and glamour of a money-spinning empire. At the end of the day they all still wear boots and kick a ball around on a pitch; the same markings and the same size.

I just hope that you enjoy the things I have to say and laugh when I laughed, maybe even cry when I cried but, most importantly, smile with me when you finish.

Read on and enjoy!

Ken Shellito
October 2018

# THE EARLY DAYS

I WAS born at home on 18 April 1940. What with the war going on the women had no choice. Most of the hospitals were full of the injured, so it would have been considered a luxury to go into hospital and give birth!

Our home was in Bartle Avenue, East Ham, not far from West Ham's football ground. I will be honest in that I can't remember the number. I don't even know if it is even still standing but it was a small terraced house, the traditional two up, two down. It had a small garden but my only memory of that was the Anderson shelter, our homemade shelter from the bombs that started dropping, courtesy of the Germans, pretty soon after I came into the world. A big hole had been dug in the garden and a corrugated iron-type shed was sunk into the hole with a set of steps going down. My memories of being carried down into the shelter are fairly clear but I don't ever remember being scared.

Maybe it was the comforting arms around me and being held close to Mum that helped me through it. I did have the company of a brother who was two years older than me but as a baby, I suppose as long as I got my milk I was happy and as the months went by and I became more mobile, it just seemed a part of everyday life.

I was five months old when the German air force, the Luftwaffe, began its massive bombing attacks on Britain.

Okay, they started on aircraft factories, airfields, radar installations and suchlike. What became known as the Blitz began on 7 September 1940 and, sadly, on the first day of the Blitz nearly 2,000 people were severely injured or killed.

The frightening part when I look back is that in eight months there were more than 70 large-scale attacks on London.

From the beginning there were 57 consecutive nights of bombing raids and I consider myself one of the lucky ones because more than a million homes were destroyed and many, many thousands of civilians killed with even more seriously injured. Until halfway through the war more women and children in Britain had been killed than soldiers.

Many families were evacuated but we were cockneys and it was not the done thing. This is our home and we ain't moving till we have to. There did come a point when things got very bad though and we were forced to spend a week in Kinross in Scotland. After our brief evacuation to Kinross we moved to a flat in Elm Park, Hornchurch, not that we had a lot to move; not much more than the clothes on our backs and a few personal items. 21A Broadway was the address and this was exciting for us as kids because we were on a hill overlooking a railway station. And I do still have the vision in my mind of a sky full of aircraft.

Okay, I didn't know which were British or which were German but as a child it looked impressive.

Our flat was above a shop and the shop in those days was Tesco's. When you think of the huge stores that we have now calling themselves Tesco's this may be one of the original stores and it was about the size of my living room now! Anyway, we had one below us. It was later bought by Lloyds Bank and we had a branch below us, and was actually where I opened my first-ever bank account when I was playing football!

Now, the flat itself was quite basic: bedroom downstairs, bedroom upstairs, bathroom, kitchen and lounge. One problem was that the flat was very close to a railway station and, yes, every time a train went by it shook! We got used to it though. Well, we didn't have a choice in the matter! Getting to the air-raid shelter was not like the old place as we had to go along the balcony, down the flights of stairs; 36 steps on a twisting metal stairway; and outside into a bit of land that was fenced off by the council that we called 'spare ground'.

Not that it was much more than a muddy allotment that each flat had as a sort of garden; it was here that we would then go down into the shelter. It was another Anderson shelter as we had before: a hole in the ground with a corrugated iron roof and four bunks underground. But to be honest we didn't think of it as a hardship. It was something you had to do; the way of life. And come to think of it, after the war we used the shelter as a store for all the rubbish and stuff that we would collect for the big bonfire on 5 November.

The kitchen was the eating area as well, no dining room to speak of, just a kitchen table. The focal point of the house was the kitchen and something that hasn't really changed in most households over the years in most corners of the world; we ate, we chatted, we joked, we had a cup of tea with our friends and my brother and I fought. In the kitchen.

We always had breakfast together in the kitchen and as far as lunch goes, well, my mother never called it lunch, it was always dinner and anything after that was tea.

Mum though was a great cook and there was always something good on the table but we used to have fun with something we called LOs. Nothing strange but always very interesting because LO stood for 'leftovers'. How the mothers coped with bringing up a family I will never fully understand.

Food was not readily available, and I do remember many times eating stale bread, softened with milk, and the milk itself was more often than not slightly off. Food rationing had begun before I was born, and each person was allowed a specific amount of basic foods. Clothes rationing began in 1941 and a new kind of 'utility clothing' was introduced, using cheap materials and the minimum amount of cloth. People were encouraged to 'make do and mend' their worn-out clothes. My mum, like most of the other mums, was actually a master with old clothes, darning socks, sewing on buttons and repairing my trousers. The hand-me-downs that I grew up in were well maintained!

Goods such as bread, alcohol and tobacco were not rationed, to keep up morale. As the war went on though, even bread became in short supply and long queues would form outside shops. Mum would always take me and my brother along with her when she had to go and queue. I think the thought of an air raid and not being with us would have been too much.

We never had a fridge at home, so everything used to go into the parlour. There was a flow of air in the parlour from a window that wouldn't shut, which kept things relatively cool!

But the air was not the only thing circulating. There were creepy crawlies and all that and I must say that some of the things Mum cooked were different. We've all had bubble and squeak, well now you know where it comes from. What with the leftovers of potatoes and cabbage and anything else, all fried up very crispy but very, very delicious. We always enjoyed our food though. I think when there is the element of survival and an unconscious thought about where and when your next meal might be, you ate what was put in front of you and you cleaned your plate – no leaving this, no leaving that.

Even if it made you feel sick, you ate everything. You daren't leave a thing!

I sometimes wonder how my mum managed everything but I come back to the camaraderie and friendship that became the norm during the war years. Everyone worked together, everyone joined together. If somebody needed help, there was always somebody there. Despite the whole tragedy of the war, the human spirit was amazing, and I can be honest and say I've never seen anything like it again. The resilience of Londoners in the face of the nightly attacks has quite deservedly passed into legend. Ordinary men, women and children showed amazing and continued courage just by carrying on with their daily lives in spite of the bombing raids.

In the end, many people became almost so immune to them that they just carried on with what they were doing. I even remember being told that some cinemas would continue to show films during raids and the audience would remain to watch them!

Some people have even credited the evolution of the 'Welfare State' to this. I still value the lessons I learnt through this time, not least the determination to succeed and the companionship of our friends.

The Germans introduced another danger to us all: we called it the Doodlebug. I am sure you have heard of it. This was a rocket-shaped machine, had flames coming out the back, and it rattled along through the air making a terrible racket.

When the noise stopped, that's when you would run like bloody hell because that meant it was coming down. One came down about a mile from us and crashed into Chase Farm House and they said the whole family was wiped out.

Even years later we used to go there to play but we were told to stay away as it was haunted. Being the little sods we were though we ignored this. Funnily enough every time we went there one of us got hurt. It was a cut knee or standing on a nail, tripping over and cutting your head and stuff. So many accidents, and after a while we did as we were told.

Did I come through unscathed? Physically, yes, but I do have a vivid memory of explosions and I think this is why I still to this day have a fear of thunderstorms. Constant noise from the bombs day after day is something very difficult to make people appreciate, especially when they haven't experienced it. I think I was blessed because I don't remember actually mourning the loss of a friend or family.

And do you know what seems crazy to me now as a child spending the first few years of my life in this situation; it was like a game to us. One of the things we found was that we didn't really know what the fighting was for and at the end of the day we was fighting for food and fighting for survival and nobody really told us what the war was about, let alone where our fathers were. Apart from when he was wounded and came back for a couple of weeks I never saw my dad for my first four years and I still wonder to this day how things would have been for me and my family if Dad had been around. I remember asking Mum on many occasions, 'Where's Dad?' and she just told me 'He is working, he is working' and nothing more was said.

As I said before, for us kids the war was really just a game and the fantastic part was that our mothers did not dispel that myth for us. With no dads around they were really all we had as our role models and better still they continued to let us believe it was a game and I thank them for that.

They didn't block the thought of a game; they didn't give us the fear of what was likely to happen or what could happen.

Because of this we didn't understand the fear and again I thank the mums for not putting that fear in us. It was a case of 'get on with it!' – blissful ignorance I think they would call it! We would always make an amusing picture as when we were outside we invariably had our helmets on. I say helmets but they were actually the old metal colanders! If we wanted to play outside we had to wear them, and they were orders from the boss, our mum! But the fun we had as we scavenged around was amazing. The amount of shrapnel was huge and we never thought what damage it may have done, the people it may have injured, or whether it was anything dangerous. We just thought about what we could do with it, what could we make? A part of the game!

You know you have got a father but during the war the only men I remember seeing were the air-raid wardens. As I said before, I did see my father once during the war but he spent that two weeks in bed getting better and then he was off again and I was still only a couple of years old! When he did finally come back for good we all went up to Victoria Station to meet him as that's where his train came in and we were there to welcome him back and take him home. I can always remember standing at the station and seeing all the soldiers walking along the platform but not actually knowing which one was my dad. Maybe my brother knew but I'd never had the chance to get to know Dad before. The funny thing was that when they were sent home they came back in what they called a 'demob' suit. They all looked the same. It was a strange feeling just standing there watching and not knowing the face I was waiting for.

People have asked me about when I did meet my father, in effect for the first time, what was the feeling? What was the emotion? Strange you might say, but there was an immediate bond. Don't ask me why as I haven't got a clue, but the bond was there. When he finally came back for good he didn't have a job and I remember sometimes he'd just say, 'Come on, let's go for a walk' and we'd go down the pub. Those days the pubs opened at 12 and closed at two and children definitely weren't allowed in. So he would sit me down on the steps outside and say, 'Stay where you are' and he would go and get me a half of bitter, but he would always say don't drink it too quick. Wise words because I was only six years old. People would look down at that nowadays I know but back then it was just the way it was.

My brother and I had also developed a knack for helping Mum. We used to climb the wall into the dairy nearby and steal the milk. Okay, it was short-lived as when the milkman caught on he got two very large dogs to watch over things.

Our local off-licence was slightly more amenable to us climbing their fence, taking the empty bottles out and then returning them to the pub off-licence to get the 1p deposit per two bottles. Not a lot but it all helped, and I am sure the guv'nor knew what was going on but he let it go. Maybe his way of helping out!

My father was also a very heavy smoker.

He smoked a brand called Weights. I could never understand why he smoked so much but I do remember the day when Dad said, 'Son, you know why they call them "weights", simple, it's because When England Invaded Germany Hitler's Troops Surrendered.' I started smoking at 14! I soon stopped though but started again later during my coaching career.

You know, the pressure and all those excuses.

Next to our flat used to be a greengrocer and it was always a laugh for us. The shop was on a hill and there would always be the table outside with the potatoes neatly stacked. Being one of those foldaway tables, it was too much temptation for us not to knock the legs from underneath and watch as the potatoes all rolled down the hill. Not that we would waste the vegetables as a few of us would be at the bottom of the hill to catch the spuds. I remember we would tuck our tops into our trousers and stuff our shirts with as many as we could then run like bloody hell around the corner.

One day while doing this prank, I think the greengrocer must have informed the police because the local PC was waiting round the corner and we ran straight into him. You would never run away from a policeman and anyway it was his beat so he knew us all! We just stopped and stood still while he spoke to us. We were bloody frightened but all he said was, 'Take them back and if it happens again I will come to your flats to tell your dads.' We knew that would hurt us a lot more than he could. That prank didn't happen again.

From my young eyes the whole world had seemed to be fighting; fighting to survive the war and, for my father now, fighting to find a job when he came home, and then fighting to keep his job. Remember, there were thousands upon thousands of soldiers returning from the war. I was only five years old when Dad returned from the war and we saw it all.

But this is where the environment that my mother and others like her created came into play. During the war, the backbone of Britain was the women. I can't think of a better way to describe it. Everything they did was for survival and they brought everybody together. It was a way of life and at the end we would still ask, 'Where are the planes?', or 'What, no more fights?' It was the attitude, the security and a safety net that the mums had created to make our lives as normal as possible.

Finally, the war was over, and I still remember to this day the soldiers coming home and all over the country there were street parties. The streets were lined with tables and piled with food and I still don't know where the food came from. But it was a big celebration and a wonderful time to be here in London. The street parties were great and the parents organised lots of games for us to play, such as egg and spoon races, with real eggs but hard-boiled so there was no waste if it dropped to the ground; wheelbarrow races, not with a proper wheelbarrow but anything with a wheel and a seat; three-legged races; chariot races; and to be honest it was anything to celebrate together ... and a great time was had by all.

# HOME IS WHERE
# THE HEART IS ...

THE HEART of the cockney way of life was always the home and it does make me smile when I look back on those times. There was always a feeling of safety and Mum was always in control, the best grounding for a young lad just itching to explore and cause mischief.

The war had toughened everybody up and educated us in one way but soon it was time for me to start some form of school education. Well, that was the idea my parents had, I think. The start of my schooling and the end of the war were quite close together, one battle to another I always say, but I started at Benhurst Avenue Primary School in Elm Park in 1945. I have a good recollection of my first day. My cousin June took me to school because she went to the same school. I walked in and being my first day I was just playing with plasticine. Anyway, I was in class and the bell goes for the end of the lesson. Being none the wiser I got up and walked home thinking school was over for the day! This is good, I thought. It was safe, hardly any cars on the road, so no real problem.

Then as I turned up the alley behind the flat, Mum was sitting with Auntie Eileen who was looking down from the balcony as I walked up the alley. 'There's your Ken coming home,' she said, to which Mum replied, of course, 'No, he's at school.'

I remember Mum looking over and shouting, 'What are you doing here?'

'School's over, the bell went,' I said.

She did laugh, and I was taken back in time for the afternoon classes! A lesson that I soon learnt!

Life at home went on as normal. Normal might be an exaggeration on my part. I don't think anything was ever normal as such. Mum and Dad were both working trying to keep food on the table, keep us kids clothed, and I suppose at the end of the day keep us all happy. Most mornings we had breakfast together: bread and milk and occasionally some fruit or a biscuit washed down with a cup of tea. Dad would leave the house first and then Mum, me and my brother would leave together. I was invariably the first home but I was never given a house key. That was attached to a piece of string inside the letter box and I would put my hand through the letter box and pull it out and unlock the door.

Just imagine doing that now!

Dad's job was called a rope runner but let me explain.

He worked at Beckton Gas Works on the trains and his job was that as his train came along to the sidings he would jump from the train, run along the track, pull the barrier up, let the train go through then chase the train and jump back on board. Not the most exciting of jobs but this time after the war a job was a job and if you didn't have a job you didn't take home any money. Mum worked as a cashier in 'Spicers' greengrocers in Beacontree. During the long school summer holidays, I would go with Mum and I actually had a small job in the back unloading delivery vans carrying the vegetables and fruit and stocking the shelves.

One of my important jobs was actually making sure that the older fruit and vegetables stayed on top so when the new stock came in I would have to take all the old veg out for the new stuff to be put at the bottom and put the old veg back on top. I did enjoy it when the grapes came in. They came in small barrels protected with a sort of cork and I remember when the grapes came in I was told to keep whistling. I soon realised that was to stop me eating them! It provided me a bit of pocket money and gave me a little bit of independence.

And then there was our neighbour, Mrs Milne. We actually called her 'nose ointment' as she always had her nose in everyone else's business. Unlucky for us kids as she knew everything and reported everything! I blame her for a number of good hidings that I got!

After the war it seemed there was always an endless supply of cement for repairs and stuff. Well, you can imagine it was another source of fun: we would cut the bags open and then bang it so that the cement dust flew out. Problem being on one occasion that I was a silly sod and was looking over the bag as it was hit! Cement dust went straight in my eyes. It didn't hurt so much but took a couple of days to be cleared. Mum had rushed me to the doctor's, so no lasting damage. Now I look back and just think 'glad there wasn't any sand with it!' That mixed with my tears would have been interesting.

My neighbour and partner in fun was Gary Weston. One day we had found a tin of paint and it was nearly full. We opened it up and I was stirring it when Gary threw a lighted match into the tin. 'Whoosh' it went and took with it my eyebrows, eyelashes and most of the hair on my forehead! It actually took ages to grow back!

Life was one big exploration and we were gonna enjoy it to the full. One of the dads had helped us make bows and arrows, something we could enjoy. You know, just a bit of cane and some string and there it was. But, that wasn't enough for us; at the back of the off-licence where we used to take bottles and get a deposit back we had noticed an old set of darts that, needless to say, didn't stay there for long.

We put them in a pocket and already had a use for them: we attached the point of the dart to the end of our arrow and put up a nice target to fire at down the end of the alley. I had taken my shot and was by the target pulling my arrow out when Gary decided to shoot again – straight into my shoulder.

It was sore but the crazy thing was, it was still just a game and 'one of those things'. We just got on with it! Just like during the war, we didn't understand danger.

While playing at the back of the shops one day, a lady who worked there came out and asked what we were doing by their store. Being a bit cheeky I noticed she had a ladder in her stocking, so I told her.

She came straight back with 'I bet you would like to climb it.'

'Silly cow,' I said, 'how can you climb a stocking?'

It wasn't too much longer before I learnt!

# THE HOME LIFE

I DO remember waking up at night sometimes with Dad coughing. I think he knew he had to quit smoking but he came back from the war with a cigarette in his mouth and God only knows what he went through when he was in the army. I mentioned before how when we have a heavy thunderstorm now I have to try and get away from it all, do something else like cooking or something. If this was an after-effect of the Blitz, I thought to myself, what the hell was it like for those guys in the trenches during the war? When lightning starts now you have to be bloody unlucky to get injured or killed, but those guys in the trenches didn't know if the next flash, the next bang was gonna be the one that killed you. I know how I react to a thunderstorm so very few know how much greater the action was in the thick of the war and how those soldiers coped.

I really do admire what my father and the many thousands of others did during this time and more so how they adjusted back to a normal life at home. A fond memory of Dad was when he decided to paper the living room ceiling.

Now bear in mind we were in a flat above a shop overlooked by another flat. As I have said before, whenever anybody had a problem or needed a hand there was always someone to help out. So, it was my good friend Gary Weston's dad, Uncle John and me dad who had removed the door from its hinges and supported it over two chairs to act like a platform. We didn't have a ladder or nothing like that. Uncle John had said to Dad to stand on the one end and hold the paper up and he was gonna work from the other end. So there was me dad holding up the paper and obviously he had to stretch. Now, he had a big belly on him and so when he stretched that went in, and of course down came his trousers. They both rolled around laughing and I remember Mum running in and she was so embarrassed. That piece of paper did eventually get done though as Dad just used a broom to hold up the paper as Uncle John worked from the other side. After that one bit the Guinness came out and that was it for the day!

That's what I loved about living in the flats, everyone was together.

In those years I can't remember actually brushing my teeth! I suppose someone must have, I mean I still have half my teeth. Other things like Mum making sure we had our daily bath, funny to think of it now but maybe every kid has a natural aversion to scrubbing themselves clean every night.

I know I did but Mum would hear nothing of it. Our hot water supply was from a geyser in the kitchen. Problem being it was coal-fired! So, we had to keep it stoked up, we had to keep it clean and during the summer months, if you wanted hot water it had to be alight. I will leave you to imagine how hot the kitchen got.

That gives me fond memories of the coalmen. We had a coal bin on the balcony and it took three or four bags of coal to fill it. There was something special about the coalmen. Our flat was above the shop and there were two flights of stairs to get up. They would climb the stairs with a heavy bag of coal on their shoulder. Up and down three or four times and they would never moan, never say a bad word. It was their job and no job meant no money. But the funny thing was, it was good luck for the coalman to touch you, so I would almost wait in anticipation for the guy to ruffle my hair and say, 'All right, son.' And it was even luckier if he gave you a piece of coal, but I never thought to ask why!

The coalman was always round our place over New Year's Eve. He would bring us a piece of coal and tell us 'this is for good luck!' He would do that for every house on the verandah and the funniest part was an interesting celebration as we used to throw the dustbins over the balcony as the clock struck midnight. I wish I knew why! But it was crash, bang and wallop all down the alley and then of course the following morning we had to go and sort out which bin was ours. Fortunately, our house number was on our bins. And talking of the dustbins, our dustmen would climb the stairs to come and collect rubbish from outside the door. Just think about the way it is now; if you don't take your rubbish out they don't collect it. Same with the milkman who would come round to every house or flat and leave the milk outside your door. No one would ever think of taking what wasn't theirs!

# THERE WAS NOTHING
# LIKE CHRISTMAS

CHRISTMASTIME WAS always fun as family was always around. Another piece of cockney heritage really. I mean, me Auntie Eileen was next door and her husband who was in the submarines during the war and her son Gary and then Auntie Ivy and Auntie Vi also nearby. And then we had a whole host of friends and it was my dad who once said, 'Friends are more important than your relatives. You pick your friends!' So Christmas was another excuse for everyone to get together.

Dad always would bring home a big leg of pork on Christmas Eve but because he would quite often have a few beers on the way home from work at Beckton Gas Works, we used to go up to the train station and meet Dad off the train. Mum said we had to make sure he didn't leave it on the train or be caught dragging it along the street!

Don't ask me how but there was always a nice meal and a bit of alcohol to enjoy. Mum's Christmas puddings were legendary; she would make them in May, so they had a lot of time to season and, with all the brandy, ferment! She would bring them to the table and then set them alight before serving. I never forget the smell was so gorgeous.

After lunch we usually went down to Auntie Vi's and she always had a Christmas tree with all the trimmings and presents below wrapped in Christmas paper. As young kids the excitement of Christmas was always fantastic. Christmas Eve we would always put a stocking at the end of our bed and Santa would always bring us some fruit and, if we were lucky, some chocolate. We actually wrote our Christmas list about a month before Christmas and every Christmas list I wrote included blue-and-white football socks! More often than not, I got a pair!

My parents, family and friends always made sure that us kids had a good Christmas, but I know that most times the money for Christmas came from the pawn shop. One of the highlights, as at most of our parties, would be my granddad playing his banjo. We never found out where he learnt or who taught him but he was bloody good. It was always a sing-along and you must remember the famous cockney tune, 'The Lambeth Walk'; we would go along the road and in and out of people's houses and flats in a long line just singing away … fantastic memories. Quite often in my Auntie Vi's flat she would accompany him on the piano and there was also a 'squeezebox', an accordion-like thing, but I can't remember who played that.

I suppose for us at this time that was our way of enjoying an evening together. I mean, there weren't TVs and CDs and stereos in our street! It was a culture that you grew up with. I must say it was good and problems, well, you never seemed to have problems because your parents kept them away from you! If they were short of money or whatever, we would never go short.

They would always find a way to make sure our life didn't change. It wasn't just in my family, it was all around and it was an attitude that people just had. I think that was a hell of a good thing.

And another strange skill my granddad had was that he could speak Arabic! And we still don't know how or why!

# REMEMBER, REMEMBER
# THE FIFTH OF NOVEMBER

NOVEMBER THE fifth and bonfire night was always looked forward to. As kids we were more attracted by the noise of the fireworks and there was never the slightest thought of causing damage or injury.

I say that because one of the things we looked on as 'fun' was putting the bangers through people's letter boxes! We were usually long gone before the residents came to the door. And more fun – or should I say noise – for us lads was putting the bangers under a metal dustbin lid. It wasn't long before we were all banned from getting hold of the fireworks. There was a small display each year, not an organised event but the parents would club together and buy Catherine wheels and rockets and stuff and the spectacle was amazing for us youngsters. The bonfires were also always very big and even the following day we would go back and cook jacket potatoes in the smouldering ashes. The mums would even make stew to go with them.

I do look back and realise how 'normal' our childhood was and what with the war and everything it still amazes me that our folks kept it that way. As for the cost, once again, the pawn shops did well!

Mum had created a home for us and it was always good to be there. It was an ever-open door and it seemed there was always food on the table. Friends and relatives would always be nearby and when they visited they would just knock on the door and come on in! Okay, I had to share a room with my brother and we didn't always get on but I wasn't ever hungry, though to be honest, I do remember being very cold during the winter. In bed at night I would usually have a hot-water bottle … well, I say 'bottle' but it was more like a clay pot. It would probably be a collector's item now. And the crazy thing was, when it was full of hot water you couldn't actually put your feet on it, so you would wrap it in a towel, which, I suppose, defeats the object!

Talking of water, the problem we did have with the flats and houses along our street during the winter were the water pipes. On a regular basis the pipes somewhere in the flats would burst. But, brothers in arms, your neighbours and people around would always come to help, along with the plumber, of course, when he arrived. Problem solved!

That team spirit again and so good to all be playing for the same team. Very similar to what I am experiencing now and the spirit of the Kadazan and the other tribal people of Sabah in Borneo. This spirit built our traditional house here in Sabah where every weekend the villagers would come up the hill to build our house; I supplied timber and equipment and they brought their own tools. They start 9am, lunch at noon, start again at one, and finish at four. That's when they have their liquid refreshment, stagger home down the hill any time they want (but more of that later), but there is never a 'how much' or 'what's it worth'? They would just up turn and get on with it.

This is how it was with the people in the flats.

I do look back on those times with affection and I think many people of my age and my era consider themselves lucky. We were never materialistic; we had what we had and that was that and we were happy to have such good friends around us.

# MY FIRST LOVE

SITTING IN a classroom would drive me up the wall and with the lack of time I spent at school I suppose I became more streetwise than being good at any academic skill. But it was at Benhurst Primary that I first started playing and fell in love with football. Before this the extent of my footballing was kicking tin cans on the street and I would remember watching my brother and his friends kicking a ball around and just wanting to play. One day, they asked me to join them and, yes, I bore the brunt of all the tackles, but I had had the time of my life. My dad was also there, quite often just watching, and on one occasion someone kicked the ball very high and I was preparing myself to head it. I heard him shout from the touchline, 'Don't head it, it will flatten you like a kipper.' Of course, I did head it and the nickname of 'Kipper' stood from that day on. Even schoolteachers called me by that name. And I never looked back. Note though that I never told anyone at Chelsea, especially Terry Venables!

Bear in mind with all that had been going on with the war there weren't many parks, goalposts, football pitches and things like that for us to play our game. Anyway, we played a lot of football, or so it seemed, while I was at primary school. We were put into four teams: red, yellow, green and blue, and we stayed with those teams until we were 11. For all the sports activities, we had inter-class matches on a Wednesday, all based on these colours with one-inch chest bands and from the inter-class matches the school team was selected. Coaching bibs were not invented then!

Saturday mornings were when we had the inter-school competition. This was on a league basis and covered all the sports: football, cricket, boxing and athletics. We had a good school team though and my good mates were there: Brian Gregory, Ronnie Dodson, Harry Woods, Don Fleetwood and Charlie King, some of whom I am still in regular contact with. I must note here that we didn't have a school bus and most families didn't have a car. There were occasions for away games where we had up to two hours' walking before we even kicked a ball. Would have been nice to cycle but it was not safe carrying football kit, boots and sometimes food. This was where my love of sport began and one of the early mentors I had was my teacher Mr Len Lloyd, who was interested in all sports and gave us all a wonderful start to these activities. I think Mr Lloyd was one of the most popular teachers but maybe that was just because his lessons were all like free time! I mean, I don't know anyone who didn't enjoy PE at school.

I must mention a bit about Dad's interest in football. He was actually a pretty good footballer himself and I remember watching him play for the Beckton Gas Works football team.

It makes me smile when I picture him going off to play football with his 'doctor's bag'. Seriously, he had his kit and boots and stuff all neatly placed in what I had only ever seen in a doctor's surgery. It did the job though. The one lasting memory, or should I say smell, when I went with Dad and they were all getting changed for their match, was 'white horse oil', a fairly pungent oil they rubbed on their legs, etc., to warm up for a match. I do remember one game with Dad running down the wing and suddenly pulling up and falling to the ground; he had cramp in both legs. As he was carried back to the changing room the crowd, albeit small, was singing 'Old Soldiers Never Die'. I was a very proud kid that night.

For me, one of the highlights of playing in the Saturday morning leagues was that my dad was always there. If he couldn't make it through work commitments, my granddad was there. They were my best supporters and Granddad used to call our team the 'ragged arse' Wanderers! By the time I was in my ninth year, all I wanted to be was a footballer. Loving everything to do with sport, I missed a lot of schoolwork! My brother would sometimes tell Dad when we got home that I hadn't been at school today. I forget the number of times I got a good hiding from Dad but in the end he actually just took me outside and we went for a walk and we talked. My father was actually quite a good footballer in his day but those days there weren't contracts and stuff like that. His ambition had been to become a footballer but it never materialised and I think this was where his early desires for his own football career and how it didn't work out came through in that he wanted to give me every opportunity to succeed. I sincerely thank him for that as I don't know how far I would have gone without him at my side.

At ten years old and with the backing and continued support of Mr Lloyd, I was selected to play for the district team of Hornchurch. And that was where I first encountered Jimmy Greaves. Jimmy played for Dagenham and even though it was only three miles from home it was like the other side of the world! The match ended 2-2 and I bet you can't guess who scored the Dagenham goals! Jimmy and I later became very good friends and you'll read more about that later.

# BACK TO SCHOOL
## ... SORT OF!

SHORTLY AFTER my 11th birthday, I had left Benhurst because I had failed my 11 plus exams – no surprise to Mum and Dad. Anyway, before I knew it I was off to Sutton's Secondary School in Hornchurch. This was another sports-mad school, so it was perfect for me and, again, I think I was very lucky because the sports teacher, Mr Crew, was another amazing role model and the encouragement he gave us all we will never forget. PE was also a favourite lesson again and the only lesson I really enjoyed outside of football and I remember one lesson when Mr Harvey, the PE teacher, wanted someone to show everyone how to do a handstand.

I offered and as I went down on my hands and raised my legs, Mr Harvey caught my ankles and I broke wind, much to the amusement of all the other classmates. 'It's a natural body function,' Mr Harvey said, as my mates laughed even more! Both Mr Crew and Mr Lloyd played a vital role in my developing passion for football. School was about an hour's walk from home and Mum did quite often give us the money for the train but we would put it in our pocket and walk all the same. I mean, there was really no traffic to worry about. It was only if the weather was really bad that we wouldn't walk.

Sutton's was different in that on the football pitch this was the first time we were given definitive roles to play. I was a very proud 11-year-old playing in the under-15s and I played right-half. It was here that I suppose I had one of my early career-defining moments. This is where I met and played football with Charlie Hurley. He was two years older than me but we played together in the under-15s and he was captain of the team. Always a good person and always the one to make you believe in your own ability and obviously someone I looked up to, both on the pitch and off. Shortly after, Charlie left school and went to Millwall. He was there as what was then called a 'ground staff boy'. In effect, the bottom of the professional footballing ladder but he was being paid and I remember thinking, 'You can actually get paid playing football?' Just hearing about Charlie made me think 'I can do this' and, maybe more relevant, 'I want to do this!' From that point on I was going to be a professional footballer. Charlie became a Sunderland legend that some of you may remember.

Sometimes I do regret not attending classes at school as much as I should have but my determination to play sports, be it football or cricket, meant that regret at that early age wasn't even a consideration. I just enjoyed going to the park and if there were lessons we didn't like we would go to the park and play football all day. Don't forget that in those days you didn't just get detention or have to stand in the corner with your head against the wall; it was the cane, and it hurt! The classrooms in those days were very strict and the cane was struck across your knuckles and if you thought of being clever and moving your hand the teacher would swing the cane back up and hit the underside. Ow!

Enough said, but I will stress that you didn't want the cane and you learnt your lesson very quickly!

By this time Mum and Dad had bought me a bike. I remember it well and it was called a Hopper Clubman. The thing about this bike was that the handlebars were an early form of the drop handlebars we always see now. It was every morning before school that I would hop on the bike and cycle to the newsagent to get the *Greyhound Express* for Granddad. Basically this was the racing news for greyhounds and as my granddad lived on the way to school I would drop it off for him. At lunchtime I would cycle back to Granddad's and I would pick up the bets he wanted to make. It does make me laugh because I can still picture him sitting there and he would pick his nose and wipe it on the newspaper and then he would pass his bet over to me and say, 'Here you are lad, let's hope I win!'

Now, at this time gambling was only allowed in the registered bookies at the tracks. Down behind the flats there was an old railway yard and in one of the old train carriages was a makeshift bookie. Don't forget I was only 11 years old!

The bookie's name was Mr Andrews and I would just pass over Granddad's bet and the cash, maybe a shilling or so, no receipts or nothing but my granddad would circle his choice and that always seemed good enough for Mr Andrews, and the bet was placed. The following morning when I picked up the next *Greyhound Express*, he would check the results and place another bet. If he had won he would ask me to deduct the next bet from the winnings and then drop the rest back to him. Funny thing was, he would always make me drop his winnings off before I went back to school! As if I would dare do anything with it.

Dad was great for me when I was at Sutton's, especially when it came to homework. The teachers gave me homework but Dad told them, 'He ain't doing that. You've got him from nine 'til four to teach. That's enough learning; the rest has got to be recreation. He is playing football!' What a dad! He wasn't always like that as when I was at primary school, he was very positive about studying hard and stuff. I suppose the change came when he saw me playing football, when he realised he really liked what he saw. My granddad also saw this and it seemed like they both set out their plans for me.

Other after-school activities included choir practice and I laugh again because so often the music teacher would say, 'Stop, stop, someone's got it wrong.' We would sing it again and I would just mime. 'That's better,' the teacher would say, so I knew it was me! More often than not after that, when choir practice was on, I was practising football. When I say 'practising football', in the playground I kicked a tennis ball around and going home it was a tin can. I hadn't played with a real football until I was seven but the inner bladder of the cheap footballs would burst, so we would fill it with paper and as there were no goalposts and no lines, we had bricks and jackets and shirts to mark the posts and we just played, played our hearts out.

One of the teachers that I have fond memories of was Ernie Roberts, our science teacher. Now, science at the best of times was boring for us but 'Mad Ernie', as we called him, made it fun. And I don't mean fun to learn; the fun part with Mad Ernie was that he would be standing there in front of us and he would fall asleep; his eyes were just shut then he would be rocking gently back and forth. He used to have a sort of pendulum behind him and if you remember the valves you would use to pump up the football, one of those was hanging on the end to keep it swinging. Anyway, each time Mad Ernie seemed to fall asleep we would shout, 'Ernie, it's stopped swinging.' That would bring him back to reality!

There was one lesson where Mad Ernie decided to show us a short movie. Now, obviously we didn't have video recorders and stuff, so it was one of the old projectors. Us lads had come prepared, with pockets full of gravel. As the lights were going out, boys and girls had to sit on opposite sides. So there we are in the dark with Mad Ernie talking to us about this and that and that was our cue as a volley of gravel left our hands. He couldn't see who had thrown it, so he turned and said, 'If you're not interested, why don't you just leave the room?' We looked at each other, shrugged our shoulders, stood up and walked out. The headmaster wasn't too happy with this and although we didn't get the cane we had a pretty stiff talking-to.

Another excuse to miss a lesson or two, usually music I might add, was actually brought about by one of the sports teachers, Mr Crew. The school had a kit room, full of stuff for sports but it also included about 30 pairs of football boots, just in case someone wanted to play but didn't have a pair.

These were the old-style boots: steel toe-caps and laces that went halfway up the shin. You wouldn't see the stars of today in anything like that! Anyway, now and again Mr Crew would catch us at break time and ask if a couple of us would clean the kit room. We didn't need to be asked twice! I think it's the same for every schoolkid: there are lessons you like and lessons you don't like. I still think though that those teachers who made it fun made learning easier.

Sport aside, I actually enjoyed history and geography, but that was about it. Some of the other lessons were fun but not in a learning way; I laugh now when I think about an old school friend, Don Fleming. We was in an English class, I think, and the teacher, Mr Walsh, said, 'Hey, Fleming, how do you say this word?' Now, the word was 'melodeon' but unfortunately Don just couldn't get his tongue round it and he was saying 'melodidon' and despite repeated attempts and roars of laughter from the rest of us it made no difference. Mr Walsh saw it differently and brought the cane out, maybe thinking Don was playing around. After five strikes on the hand I think he realised Don just couldn't say it. To me that was crazy teaching and a lesson that I took with me into my footballing: don't force people to do things they cannot do. From that day on though, Fleming was always called 'Melody Don'!

We had our street teams at the weekends, and it didn't matter whether it was Saturday or Sunday, any time was football time. I remember Elm Park Avenue, Ben Hurst Avenue, Northwood Avenue, Woodcote Avenue, Warren Drive, Eyhurst Avenue, and the list goes on! Those street tournaments were amazing fun. There were no refs and no lines. The first team to arrive would put up some makeshift posts and the last team would take them down. We played our hearts out and there was always laughter, shouts and cheers, not to mention many scrapes and cuts from the grassless pitches, and the all-too-common over-excited tackle.

What many people don't know is that I was a pretty good cricketer as well. My highest score was 102 not out.

This was in the inter-district school match, but I must say that our cricket pitch was a cemented strip covered with coconut matting and to score on this was easy, especially as the bowler tried to spin the ball, making it easy for me to pile on the runs. The following week I was bowling and got nine wickets for nine runs. For that brief period, I was a bit of a hero at school!

Boxing was another sport played at school, but I was always small for my size and weight so whenever we had inter-school competitions my opponents were always taller than me. One time this guy kept hitting me with a straight left in the face. When the bell rang, I sat in the corner and cried. I wasn't picked again!

# AND ROMANCING ...

I HAVEN'T yet mentioned girls. I mean, girlfriends at that age were ugh! If you had a girlfriend you didn't take part in sport, as simple as that. They were just pushed to one side.

When I first started at Sutton's, the classes weren't mixed. I mean, there was a bit of mistrust if you were sitting at the back with a girl, you know. But it was only a short while after I started that the classes became mixed. I started Sutton's in the Easter just after my 11th birthday. I suppose the official start of the school year was in August after the summer break, which was usually about six weeks.

I started early mainly because I just wanted to get out of primary school. I think many of us did.

Anyway, it was the start of the school year proper in August 1951 that classes became mixed. Girlfriends were still an inconvenience and even when we had lessons together it was still viewed as a bit sissy to have a girlfriend.

You would play netball or play hockey with the girls but to walk hand in hand was definitely being a sissy! Okay, some boys did but this was where I could honestly say the phrase 'behind the bike shed' began. It was here that I first set eyes on Patricia. We had been in the same class for quite a while and maybe the attraction was more a shared view on what was important.

I mean, I lived for sport, while Patricia lived for her studies.

May sound a strange shared view but it was actually a shared determination: me determined to play sport and her determined to study! I was about 14 when I spoke to another lad, Colin Johnson, I think, and asked him to ask Patricia if I could walk her home. Man up, I hear you say, but that was just the way it was done. She said yes! You could say I wasn't thinking clearly because Pat lived the other side of school to me. Not the ideal courtship but everyone else was doing it, so it just happened. Okay, there was no regularity to it and we would only meet up probably once a week but I do remember how much we enjoyed chatting and I will be honest, I don't have any memory of our first kiss!

Her dad, Charlie, was in the St John's Ambulance and I liked him. He was a nice guy. I think her dad's profession was where her medical ambitions developed. Her mum Alice was also a lovely lady.

As partnerships/relationships go, it developed very slowly. Most days I would get home from school and I invariably wouldn't be going out. After having my usual kickabout it was a bath, food and then bed. I still had to get up early. So Pat was my first regular girlfriend. I did have a couple of others and I do remember their names, but Pat was really the only one that I had the time and patience for. And I think she had the time and especially the patience for me!

I mean, she would never say anything like 'Oh, so you're off down the park, what about me?'

She was actually very supportive of my dream to be a footballer. It makes me laugh now as I think I was quite supportive of her and her dreams. She wanted to be a nurse and so there were times when she wanted to practise bandaging. I'm sure you can imagine me sitting there with my head bandaged, my arms bandaged, as well as my legs, fingers and toes! But I was happy to do it. She needed the help and I was there to give it. There was no bossiness or anything like that, just two good friends just helping each other out.

# THE BEAUTIFUL GAME

SOMEBODY ONCE said that football was created by the working class for the working class and this is one of the reasons that most football stadiums are built in the working-class areas. This made it easier for the supporters to come to a game. As I was born 400 metres from West Ham's ground, in many ways it was the first team I followed.

It was also Dad's team and I very nearly signed for them as a ground staff boy at 15. I was taken into the office and Mr Ted Fenton was there, the manager. I was with my dad and they interviewed me as a potential ground staff boy. As we walked in and sat down, Mr Fenton locked the door! And I didn't like that, I didn't like that at all! I sat and I listened to him talk about the team, you know, my dad's team and my team, but I didn't like that. After, my dad looked at me and said, 'What do you think?' We never went back. I thought it was the wrong thing to do, and I never found out why he locked the door!

The principle he had was 'you're in and you don't leave until I let you'. Not for me!

Sutton's gave me a fabulous grounding in football. Even though I had started football a little later than most, I played for the school team, the district team, the county team and

London schoolboys. I know my father was the proudest dad on the touchline.

I mentioned before how I had met Jimmy Greaves when he was playing for Dagenham as a schoolboy. We caught up with each other again when we both played for Essex schools. It was 1954 when we were in the southern counties tournament and the last game for the championship was against Hertford. We won the match and we also knew there were a lot of scouts from the big teams, the professional teams outside. We all wanted to stick together and I remember Jimmy saying to us all, 'Where should we go?'

It was another team-mate who said his favourite colour was blue, so we decided on Chelsea – as easy as that!

# THE BOTTOM OF
# THE CHELSEA HILL

BEING FROM the East End, Chelsea was the other side of London but it was only a few days later when we met the chief scout for Chelsea, Mr Thompson, under the clock at Liverpool Street Station. Now the world of signing for a football club was very different in the 1950s; signing-on fees, agents, press conferences and the like were not heard of. We met the chief scout, we travelled to Chelsea's ground and we signed the apprenticeship forms.

A big disappointment for me on a day that turned out to be the start of my career was that my father was unable to join me, but to be honest it was my fault as I needed his shoes. They were the only men's shoes in the house and were shared between Dad, Terry, and me and as it was important for me to look good, I wore them, so Dad went to work. The shoes were used for other things as well. They were used by me as football boots; I would put the shoes on the hobby foot and knock in the studs. After the game, when I arrived home, I had to pull out the studs with pliers and then knock matchsticks into the holes, rub them over with sandpaper and clean and polish them. If they were wet I had to pack the shoes with old newspaper, leave them by the stove to dry and polish them the next day until you could see your face in them. Jimmy's dad was also unable to attend due to work. But we had each other, and I suppose this was the beginning of our great friendship.

I mentioned before when Charlie Hurley left to sign for Millwall and how he signed on as a 'ground staff boy', well, that was just what we were at Chelsea. Our first day at work was short; we all signed the forms, were shown around the ground, were taken to lunch and then went back home.

# A WORKING LIFE BEGINS

YOU MUST bear in mind that I was just coming up to 15 years old and at 15 you could leave school if you had a job to go to, so I was off! Pat, who was still my regular girlfriend, stayed on for maybe eight or nine months more. She then went straight into nursing at a local hospital and I remember her having a lot of studying to do. That was right up her street though. She loved to study and like with anything she did, failure was not an option. Her determination to be a nurse was just like my determination to be a footballer.

My life was just starting as well. I was now a ground staff boy at Chelsea. The contract we had signed was to start at nine in the morning, lunch was from 12 until one and then we finished at four. After that it was training. And best of all our pay was £2, 16 shillings and one penny per week – an absolute fortune! To get to work by 9am, I had to leave home by 6.45am. As we were mainly from the East End of London, we would get the district line. Many of the ground staff boys would get on the same train on the journey to Fulham Broadway but I remember my journey was probably the longest. I was the furthest down the line and had 33 stations to go through, which would take about an hour and 30 minutes. Not surprisingly, I can still remember all the stations! On the way home it was Brian Legg and Derek Winn who got off at Aldgate East, Jimmy would get off at Mile End with Mike Harrison, then Billy Wall at Upton Park, Dennis Long at Barking and Brian Dellar at Dagenham Heathway before I got off at Elm Park.

As juniors we had to work at the main ground at Stamford Bridge all day. We worked in pairs and our duties were split up to the various areas where we were needed: one pair in the dressing room, one pair in the office, one pair in the snooker room and two pairs on the ground. The others would be training at the Welsh Harp, the training ground and for those working we would all do some training after we finished at four. Each week we changed around and the workers became the trainers and vice versa. I still remember my first day of training: I was given the ball, faced the wall, later referred to as the shooting box, and our coach Mr Foss demonstrated the art of passing and then left me there passing back and forth against a brick wall for two hours.

Other boys were practising their dribbling, some practising their shooting, while others focused on the long pass and controlling the ball. It may sound mundane and boring but these different exercises were vital, and it also develops the discipline to practise.

To think of how youngsters today are treated when they are signed to a club, it's a whole different world. You could say that our apprenticeship in the 1950s was to learn our football from the grass roots up, literally! The work routine was itself a discipline. Dressing room duty was to put out training kit, make sure the training boots were clean, the footballs pumped up and laced correctly, and then after the training we had to pick up all the dirty kit when the players had left, take it to the laundry room and then return and scrub out the dressing room and clean all the boots again.

Now when I say 'clean the boots' I don't mean just wipe off the mud; they had to be wet-polished and as clean as the soldiers in red. And the other thing with the boots was to sort out the studs. In those days we had short or long studs depending on the weather; no such thing as rubber-moulded soles like now, and we had to make sure the right studs were in. Fridays was different in that the players didn't wear boots.

They would all wear spikes as their training was just doing sprints – didn't want to risk an injury for Saturday's game!

The team sheets were also put up on a Friday. The first team, the reserves and those in the third team were all up on the board late in the morning after training. Our work didn't finish with the team on Friday as we had to prepare things for the games the following day. For a team travelling away there would be two skips to pack but we always had guidance and instruction from the kit man. Before we could go home everything was inspected and once it was clear and you had your arrangements for the junior game the following day, it was time to go home. By the time I did walk through the door at home I was invariably exhausted and definitely slept well every night.

# SUN, RAIN ... AND SNOW

AT THE training ground there was no heating in the dressing rooms. One solution we did find was an old metal barrel we had banged holes in, filled with coal and set alight. Yes, we were warmer but the smell was terrible! Having the odd tea break was also allowed but I do remember seeing Jock the grounds man stirring the large teapot with a stick from outside. Other jobs that were seemingly impossible included rolling a frozen pitch; up and down we went but to be honest I don't think it made a bleeding difference, it was still bloody hard and we were all frozen stiff. Talking of which, one night after washing our kit, we hung it out to dry in the boiler room. When we returned the following morning everything was as stiff as boards!

The junior games on Saturday were at the Welsh Harp training ground if at home, and if the game was away we would all meet at Stamford Bridge for the team bus. Kick-off was always 11 o'clock but after the morning game we had to return to Stamford Bridge to do the dressing room duties for the first team or the reserves. Saturdays were always our longest day; leaving home at 7am and sometimes not returning home before eight in the evening.

Monday mornings were never fun because that was when we started sweeping the terraces, if that was our duty that week.

I'm sure you can imagine the litter, the papers and the rubbish left by the supporters from the Saturday fixtures.

Not only that but we had the ashtrays on the backs of seats to clean out. This could take two or three days sometimes and included other duties like washing the seats, cleaning the directors' box, scrubbing toilets and polishing the taps.

And you wouldn't believe the mess the pigeons would make!

For some reason, especially around the directors' box there was also a lot of brass: brass railings, brass doorknobs, brass everywhere, and this had to be spotless and gleaming.

If it wasn't we had to stay until it was done. The one benefit though of sweeping the terrace was that many people were careless with the loose change in their pockets and it was a rare day when we didn't pick up some coins.

We had two grounds to prepare for Saturday matches: one was the main ground and the other was our junior ground at the Welsh Harp.

The ground duty involved washing the goalposts, the nets and the corner flags and basically checking that everything looked good. This was not quite as easy as it sounds as we had no ladders. One day at the junior ground, the groundsman, Jock, decided to bring the jeep over for us to stand on while we cleaned the crossbar and posts. It would have been okay, except that Jock reversed too fast and hit the goalpost. Down it came. Naturally, Jock didn't do that again!

Washing goalposts and nets was a nightmare during the winter months. Our fingers became numb and stiff as we did not have plastic gloves them days, so we just had to get on and do it. Jimmy was invariably my partner and I still remember one Friday at The Bridge while we were washing the nets: freezing temperatures, wet rags in freezing water, and using Vim to clean, so our hands and fingers were stiff and sore.

Jimmy turned to me and said, 'Sod this, I'm going to get in the first team. Just look, the first team are only doing their sprints and then they are finished, I want some of that soon.'

Sure enough, two weeks later he was called over and told, 'You're playing against Spurs tomorrow, go and do your sprints!' He was only 16. Problem being that possibly left me alone, but if anything it gave me even more determination to succeed. Funnily enough, the following day Jimmy scored but even with this he was still back to his ground staff duties on Monday morning.

One of the jobs that we had to do during the 'working' week was cleaning the snooker room that the players used after training and where the families of players used to wait after the matches. One day when Jimmy and I had worked hard and made sure everything was polished, the tables swept, the seat covers ironed and basically everything perfect, Bobby Smith, a reserve team player, had started to play. He was a nice guy and he joked about our housework ability. Anyway, Ken Armstrong was the first team captain and he came in and said he wanted to play. When Bobby refused, Armstrong said he was captain and he could do what he wanted. An argument started and Armstrong picked up the coal scuttle and basically emptied it over the table, saying if he couldn't play nobody could. Bobby left the room and went down to the office. It took us ages to clear it all up and I have other not-so-fond memories of that coal scuttle as well because it had to be gleaming every day! A few days later we read the headlines that Bobby Smith had transferred to Spurs.

The training ground at Welsh Harp was also another area that needed to be kept in order and clean. The junior games were played there, and we were still expected to make sure everything was shipshape. There also wasn't any heating at the training ground, so it was always better working at Stamford Bridge because we were warm. But those days were good. We trained so we were fit and we worked hard and developed an unwavering loyalty and respect for the people in charge and for the club. This was our opportunity to succeed and the written rule was that if you weren't good enough to sign as a professional by 17 years of age you were gone. Sometimes you might get an extra year if they believed you still had a chance of reaching their targets but more often than not, 17 was the cut-off!

All the time I was gaining fantastic experience and particularly while I was playing in the Chelsea junior team in the Southeast Counties Divisions One and Two Junior League. The games were played on a Saturday morning and the league consisted of all the London clubs in both divisions. It was at this time that I played against some of the future greats of the English game: from West Ham there was Bobby Moore, Geoff Hurst, Martin Peters, Harry Redknapp and John Lyall; from Fulham, George Cohen; and from Arsenal, Liam Brady. In my own team there was Jimmy Greaves, Mel Scott, Peter Bonetti, Barry Bridges, Mike Harrison, Bobby Tambling, Terry Venables and Bert Murray.

The list was actually endless!

There were times when you would get promoted to the third team who played in the Metropolitan league. Non-league teams like Didcot, Windsor, Tunbridge, Dunstable, Hastings and Crawley, to name a few, played a part in the Metropolitan league. It was a good grounding for us to get promoted, even if it was just for the one match. Training at Welsh Harp though meant you had to carry your own boots. We couldn't wait to be full professionals training at The Bridge and to have our boots packed for us. Despite the fun we had in these games, there was still a definite desire to get to the top.

Our medical man, Dick Spence, would always give us a laugh.

He was an ex-first team player who got injured but with Spencey it was always a joke a minute. There was one game where he was strapping a guy called Brian Abery who had a weak ankle. Plenty of jokes going around the dressing room and anyway Spencey does his bit and says, 'Okay, Abes, off you go!' Abery didn't move, so Spencey asked again. Then Abes told him, 'You've strapped the wrong bleeding ankle!' This is what the game was like then. Now, it is so professional I don't know if you would have any of these little stories.

One big difference with how the game is played now is with regards to the substitutes. Whatever team you were in, if you were marked as a reserve, the only way you got to play is if one of the other players was sick or injured before the game. Otherwise you sit on the bench in your civvies, pour the tea out at half-time and at end of the game, collect all the tie-ups so they will get washed and used again for the next match and pack the skip. There were no substitutes to bring on during the game, if someone was injured during play you played with ten men!

Playing in the Chelsea juniors, I was a regular and I remember every Easter we would go on a European tour.

My second European trip was in 1958 and the tournament was played in Germany for the under-18s. I had come home one night after training and said to Dad I was picked for the European tour.

'Where are you going?' he asked.

'Germany,' I replied.

'No, you're bloody well not,' was his response.

'What do you mean?'

'You're not going to Germany!'

'But Dad, I am learning, it is just football.'

'Look! I spent six bloody years trying to kill them and they spent six years trying to kill me! And you're now telling me you wanna play football with them?'

Mum then joined in the conversation. 'Come on, Fred, you let him play against West Germany at Arsenal with the London schoolboys.'

'That's different,' Dad said, 'that was in London!'

Mum and I won the day and I did go on the tournament. This was the start of what I would call a glorious period in my life. I was fit, I was healthy and, fortunately for me, I was playing well.

One of the important memories was the FA Youth Cup Final in 1957 against Wolves. It was then played over two legs and in the first leg at home we won 5-1. The second leg we lost 6-1. An absolute disgrace by us and some of us felt that we had let Chelsea, as well as ourselves, down. But what hurt more for those of us who cared was the small group who just said, 'The game is over, why worry?' It was a carefree attitude that still riles me today. Maybe it is divine justice but those guys without the pride never made it to the big time!

# ABOUT HALFWAY UP

A SPECIAL day for me was shortly before my 19th birthday when I got the nod to play for the first team in my first league game. It was against Nottingham Forest away and we won 3-1. Best of all, I got a pat on the back from the boss, Mr Drake, the Chelsea manager. I say this was my first game in the first team, which is not exactly true, but the one other game I had was a few months before, against a South African team. The Notts Forest game was my first league game. Greavsie scored as well. I remember the game well; it was a Wednesday night, but I remember it more because I didn't kick the ball for the first 20 minutes.

Instead, I did what the boss told me to do: covering, watching the line, etc. Can you imagine it though: I am nearly 19 and playing football under floodlights and in front of a crowd of nearly 18,000 people and you win away from home. It was fantastic. I wanted more!

My direct opponent in this game was Stewart Imlach.

Now, Stuart was a good player and one thing he was good at was his movement off the ball. He was always going up and down the line and my job was to make sure he did not get behind me. We did not have a pass-over system them days, so after 15 minutes I hadn't had a kick but nor had Stuart, so I was quite content. A few minutes later the ball runs out for a goal kick and as I picked up the ball and rolled it to Bill Robertson, the Chelsea keeper, he turned to me and said, 'You take it, I am knackered.' Bloody hell, I thought, here's me running up and down like a blue-arsed fly and you say you're knackered! A bit later, Bill and I became good friends and it was a very sad day when he passed away.

After the game though the press was saying 'well done, Ken' and I had some good write-ups. But, football being football, when I looked up at the team sheets that Friday I was not in the first team, not even in the second team but back in the thirds! I was back in the Metropolitan league, playing against Didcot and what was more surprising was that nobody said a thing. It doesn't matter how you dress it up, the fact is I wasn't playing!

Mr Drake would put the team sheets up on a Friday while we were training, so by the time you got back and saw the team you were in he was usually gone. You couldn't say anything to anyone or ask someone why, even if you wanted to. And anyway, it wouldn't help matters talking.

But Mr Drake was like that! You know what I'm going to say though. I think to myself, I'm not putting up with this and I'm going to do something about it. It's not good enough and it drives you on even harder! As a youngster you want to succeed and you've had a taste of the first team and you want more.

No question about it, it was up to me. Going down to Didcot and thinking, cor blimey, it's hard! Damn, I wanted to be in that first team and as I always knew, if you get knocked down you bloody well get up again and get on with it. You've gotta get it yourself and if you don't get up, you don't get on and to be honest if the manager has to tell you that, you haven't got it in you. If no one says anything to you it's no good sitting down and feeling sorry for yourself as it's gonna get you nowhere.

You could say I was refining my game in the reserve team during this time and it seemed an age before I got my next first-team game, which was the following year against Blackburn. I was now fairly comfortable in my position at right-back, having started in that role in the youth team when the coach moved me from centre-back. I remember saying to him, 'But I've never played there.' But he just said, 'Give it a go, son!' And I did! The coach gave me the encouragement and also taught me to defend as an individual. I don't mean being selfish on the field or anything like that – it was just how he taught me to be responsible and that I had a very clear job to do, basically defend!

The good thing about turning professional was that your ground staff duties were over and that was wonderful motivation to get on. When I think back it was us kids that pulled the electric cable all along behind the shed for the floodlights and that was bloody hard work. Those cables were really heavy. People have said it was slave labour, like Oliver Twist. I disagree; if you want to succeed and it's just put on a plate for you, what's the point? One of the other summer jobs we had to do was weeding the pitch. With the pitch marked out with string, you start from one end and go all along to the other end with a small fork that you would eat your food with, digging out the weeds. The groundsman Harry Winston would always be around making sure it was done correctly.

Too many players nowadays are spoon-fed, and I still wish that back in England they did work harder at creating, nurturing and developing those youngsters that have the ability. It's all too easy though to find the talent overseas!

# NO MORE
# CLEANING BOOTS

AS A professional my salary was £12 a week at the start; match bonuses were £2 for a win and £1 for a draw. The FA had set the salary cap and it worked to the benefit of the clubs as well. It was Johnny Haynes playing for Fulham who was the first £100-a-week player. Sounds pathetic in relation to today's game!

After the Blackburn game I played two more and it was against Wolverhampton Wanderers that I received another lesson. We were defending a corner and I was on the near post and Peter Broadbent, the Wolves player, stood on my foot as the ball came over. I couldn't move but we did clear it and I remember saying 'That's not fair.' He looked at me, smiled and said, 'You'll learn.'

One day, Greavsie and I were going down Fulham Road to the pictures. As we were a bit early, we crossed the road and went into the Queens Elm pub for a quick half of bitter.

As we entered we noticed a few first-team players sitting at the bar. There was Peter Sillett, his brother John and Bill Robertson.

Peter asked, 'What are you doing in here, lads?'

'Just having a quick beer before the film starts,' we said.

NO MORE CLEANING BOOTS

'Okay.' Peter then called the barman over and told him, 'Two halves of bitter for these two lads.'

We stayed with them just chatting and Peter turned to me and said, 'Ken, you will take my place soon, so don't ruin the prospects of a good career living in pubs like me. Both of you will be internationals one day, so don't let yourself or Chelsea down.'

I owe a lot to those three men. I am not saying I don't drink beer because I do but their whole attitude towards young players who were just starting was invaluable. The advice I got from them on the ups and downs of professional football and the great stories they told gave me a great understanding of what it was gonna take to be successful.

I remember once talking with big Peter about a game I was watching and I remember an incident that included Peter. The match was against Sunderland and one of their stars was Len Shackleton, who was a class player on his day but also a bit of an individualist. Well, he was on the ball just outside the Chelsea penalty box; he looked up and just chipped the ball into the top corner of the net. I saw Peter go up and shake his hand and as he came away from Shackleton, Peter was smiling.

I asked him why he was smiling, and he replied, 'Ken, I shook his hand and said, "Great goal."'

Shack's answer was, 'Not really, Pete, I meant to get the rebound off the crossbar!'

I have never seen or heard anything like it since.

Games were obviously home and away: sometimes travelling by coach, sometimes by train. The train journeys were always fun as we'd meet early at a local café for eggs on toast before travelling to the game for the three o'clock kick-off. On the trip back to London we would always end up, if there was time, with fish and chips wrapped in a bit of newspaper. If that wasn't possible we still got five bob of food money.

By 1960 I was a first-team regular and basically the right-back position was mine. It may sound weird when you look at today's game but up to the 60/61 season the formation played at Chelsea was 2-3-5 – and that was not two up front! Let me try and explain how we defended, in effect with only two defenders. The way we had to defend was on a swivel system, where both full-backs had to come round to cover the centre-half. The idea, I think, was to make the opponents play negative passes, and not forward passes.

I feel today's formations make it more interesting for the fans and players. Would you believe, as a full-back in those days, the manager would not allow me to cross the halfway line?

I remember when the changes came in football regarding formations and systems, it was like a breath of fresh air to all concerned. But more about that later.

It was also around this time that Terry Venables joined as a ground staff boy and we seemed to hit it off well from the start.

# OUR FIRST CAR

THE CROWNING moment at this time was during the summer break after the 60/61 season when me and my mates bought a taxi. It was a hilarious purchase. Every Saturday night it seemed a regular thing to be having a beer or two at the Hinds Head pub. Anyway, we'd come out of there and turned up the road to get to the station, Chadwell Heath.

From here we'd get the train to Romford and from Romford get a taxi home. This one particular night we got a taxi and asked to be taken to Elm Park. There was me, George Delmonte, Dave Acklin and Harry Woods, my old primary school buddies.

We got to Elm Park and asked, 'Okay, how much?'

'Nothing,' said the taxi driver.

We were confused. 'What do you mean?'

'The taxi is ten years old tomorrow and it can't go on the road any more except as a private vehicle,' the driver explained. 'I've got to sell it.'

Maybe it was the beer talking but before I knew it I had asked, 'How much you want for it?'

The reply was a pretty fast '50 quid.'

I think we thought for all of a second and then asked his address and said we would see him in the morning. The taxi driver drove off and without a further word on the taxi we all went home.

Sunday mornings were always at George's house where we would play cards. We all met there, and I asked, 'What about this taxi then? Come on, its only £12.50 each.'

George, as usual, said he didn't have £12.50 but I wasn't gonna let this opportunity slide, so said I would lend it to him. One thing about George, he always paid his debts!

We went to the taxi driver's home, paid him his money and left in the taxi. Okay, not quite as straightforward as that because Dave was the only one with a driving licence! But he got us home safely. The taxi driver had told us that this was a good car but his words of warning were 'don't bash it' and 'don't speed in it'.

As I said, we made it home safely but then thought, where are we gonna park it? I mean, none of us had a driveway and we couldn't park on the street. The solution was quite simple, and convenient: it was in the pub car park opposite Dave's house. It didn't take long for the Chelsea stickers to be stuck on the doors and the back windscreen sticker that said, 'Don't laugh, mother, your daughter might be in here!'

It became a very well-known wagon and regularly on Saturday nights as we left the pub, the chorus of 'Where's the party?' accompanied our departure. And it was surprising how many people and how much beer we could fit in our taxi. I think our record was ten people in the back and five crates of beer in the front luggage bit. The taxi was also used to bring Mum, Dad, Dave and anyone else up to Chelsea when I played at home. It would always be parked at the Wheatsheaf pub, very convenient for Terry Venables and I as we would come out the ground, cross the road, go past the Rising Sun and on the way to the Wheatsheaf, which was just on the left up the hill. But it was great to walk in the Wheatsheaf as a lot of fans were walking with us chatting about the game, as we were signing autographs and got pats on the back and greetings such as 'Good game, lads', 'Not so good today, hope for better next week', or 'Here, have a beer'. A lovely way to end the day.

It was one night when the taxi was parked at the pub opposite Dave's that we decided to give it a good clean-up.

All the doors were open, the bonnet, etc., and suddenly we heard a police siren and two cop cars came roaring into the car park. Someone made a report that we was stealing this car!

They asked for the licence and documentation and Dave said, 'It's across the road at home.' At which point Dave's neighbour came out and apologised as he'd looked out of the upstairs window, seen the figures around the car and thought it was being nicked! The police saw the funny side of it.

We had the taxi for about three years but even at the end I still didn't have my licence. My one experience behind the wheel would probably put me in prison today.

Dave had suggested I learn to drive, so I ended up behind the wheel with him giving me the instructions, talking through the connecting slide window, on the clutch, the gears and so on. I stalled it once but that was because when he said 'stop', I took both feet off and put the handbrake on!

I was chuffed when I finally got the car moving.

So away we went up George's road. Then Dave said, 'Okay, turn left here', along his road and I remember joking, 'Where do you want dropping off?' They all laughed and I then moved into top gear at all of 25 miles an hour.

Dave then said, 'Junction ahead, change down to third, good, down to second, touch the brake … the brake! Touch the effing brake!'

To which I replied, 'I can't find the effing brake!'

It was then that I heard the car doors slamming and I turned to see that they'd all jumped out. Okay, I was only doing about 15 miles an hour but the junction was getting very close, so they'd abandoned ship and left me to it.

Fortunately, it wasn't too busy, so I managed to take the corner okay without further damage, except to my pride. I eventually found the brake and stopped in the middle of the road.

Looking back, it was a stupid thing to do but we hadn't set out to cause any trouble; it was more a case of being totally unaware of the possible dangers. When the guys caught up with me I said, 'No more, I'm not driving.'

It was almost six years or so before I did get my licence. Just before my son Peter was born, I took some lessons, passed my test and became the proud owner of a Ford Anglia, my first car. We did have a lot of fun in the taxi though, and for 50 quid it was a very worthwhile investment.

# ONE BIG FAMILY
# AND MY SECOND HOME

ON BOXING Day, just before the big freeze, we were playing away at Luton. Mum, Dad, George and Harry all came to the match with Dave driving the taxi. During the game, heavy snow started to fall and at half-time the lines even had to be swept. We finished the game 2-0 winners and that put us five points clear at the top. Them days with only two points for a win it was a great way to finish the year.

As we were boarding the coach to come back, Tommy Docherty said there will be a party at the Montana Hotel for all of us. I said that me mum and dad and friends are following the coach back to Stamford Bridge, so they would take me home.

They all got invited as well, plus all the other friends and parents who were at the game. Anyone who knew Tommy will tell you that on occasions like this everyone will enjoy themselves. This was no different and I have often asked how we got home as even our driver Dave does not know.

The big freeze stayed put and I think it was seven weeks before any football was played in England. Our training ground was unplayable, so we used to go to different gymnasiums for training but that was only good for fitness.

Nothing could be done for match play training, so we were stuck. Tommy then came up with the idea to go to Malta for some games. Off we went, but as it turned out there had been a lot of rain in Malta, so good playing surfaces and even football fields were hard to find. At one game the field was very sandy and where the rain had drained away it left ruts in the ground – guess who found one! I was just running along then, wallop, right foot on the edge of the rut and over I went. It was bloody painful, and I sat and watched the rest of the game. Afterwards they took me to what used to be a military hospital run by nuns, strapped me up and sent me back to the hotel. One of the sisters from the hospital lent me a walking stick, to be returned when no longer needed.

I am sure Harry Medhurst returned it as soon as I no longer needed it but I never found out if he did.

One thing I will always remember from my early playing days at Chelsea was the spirit at the club and how it was another family for me. We trained, we played and we went out together. We knew each other's strengths and weaknesses, likes and dislikes. And that reminds me of a pre-season tour to Germany.

We were staying at a big old guest house and the caretaker was an old guy with a bit of a club foot who was telling us about a British pilot who had been shot down in the war. This had happened near the hotel and so as the conversation went on we were twisting things around and spicing the story up a bit with, you know, ghosts and all that.

Anyway, we could see that Eddie McCreadie was getting a bit twitchy, as this sort of thing didn't sit well with him. Bobby Tambling had a pair of black pyjamas, so we sent him up and he stuffed the pyjamas and hung it behind the curtains in Eddie's room, leaving the window open. Eddie was downstairs with us, so he hadn't a clue. The plan was that Eddie would go up, feel a breeze and then go to the window to close it, draw the curtains and the 'body' would be there.

Well, that's what happened.

There was Terry, George, Bob and myself with Eddie when he said he was going to bed. 'You okay up there on your own?' we asked him.

He said, 'Yeh, I'm alright, goodnight.'

We were sitting there just waiting. Then came the bloody scream. If we hadn't been the only ones in the hotel it would have woken everyone.

Eddie came flying down the stairs and he was scared stiff. Even when we told him what we had done, he said he wasn't going back in there and he was sleeping with one of us! I was sharing a room with Terry and as we went up Eddie jumped in front and lay on my bed.

Eddie refused to leave and told me to sleep on the floor because he wasn't going back to his room. He never did, and I had an uncomfortable night on the floor.

Terry's antics never stopped, and you could say he was the master of the prank. One of the guys had pulled a hamstring at training one day and he had to go back to the main ground for treatment. Well, Terry had suggested that the best way to protect a pulled hamstring for the walk back was actually to walk backwards – and the player did! Then there was the airport trick we had perfected. You are sitting in the airport before your flight and obviously you will always get people running back and forth, maybe late or whatever.

Anyway, as one of these people ran past we would throw a coin or two on the floor. It worked every time: they would stop, feel in their pockets and then look around for the coins.

Another one was the 10-bob note attached to a piece of cotton. It was a natural reaction for those poor souls walking to their flight and seeing the note on the floor. Stop, bend down and try to pick it up. A tug on the cotton and away it goes.

People might look down on this, but it was our sense of humour, it was what made us laugh. Some of the victims got annoyed but most just laughed with us!

# TIME FOR A CHANGE

I HAD now secured my first-team place but unfortunately Chelsea were relegated in the 61/62 season. Liverpool were promoted! It was 1961 when Tommy Docherty decided if we were going down we would go with players who he hoped would bring us straight back up.

Docherty knew we were going to get relegated and even with a lot of games left he made a conscious decision that things had to change. He literally wiped out all the senior players from the team and brought in all us kids to complete the transformation. He could see that with the current set-up we were going down, and he wasn't afraid to stamp his authority and change things. He also brought Dave Sexton into the set-up. I used to say that Tommy was the driver and Dave the navigator.

He felt that it would be better to give the 'young guns' a chance at some first-team football in preparation for getting promotion back to the first division next season. His thinking was to go down with a group of players who would be in a position to bounce back up the following season. And that's what he done and it worked.

My good friend Jimmy Greaves had actually moved on by this time. An offer had come in to the club from an Italian team – AC Milan – and it was for £100,000, which is peanuts in the context of today's game but a fortune at that time. Jimmy was a phenomenal goalscorer, but this was still a very high fee for any player. Chelsea said no! They said they wanted £99,999! The manager, Mr Drake, didn't want Jimmy to be the first £100,000 player, so he dropped the price by £1! I don't know why Mr Drake done it but that's just the way he was. Jimmy moved on but he didn't enjoy it in Italy. He only lasted about six months. But when you think about it, how many British players have survived that much longer in the Italian game?

So anyway, Jimmy was not part of Docherty's master plan, but I don't think they would have got on. Greavsie was unique and a very good friend of mine but he didn't like training. He'd say, 'Just gimme the ball, I'll score the goals for you!' I did miss him and there are lots of stories I could tell.

I remember a game up in Newcastle. It was winter time and to play in Newcastle at that time of year was not nice.

We lost 2-0 and we were in the changing room after the game with Mr Drake looking at each of us, not impressed and he says, 'Where's Jimmy?'

A little voice from the bathroom then said, 'I'm in the bath, boss.'

'What you doing in there?' Drake asked.

Jimmy responded, 'It's bloody freezing out there, boss!'

'You've had 90 minutes to run around and get warm!'

Then Jimmy put his head round the door and said, 'You know me, boss. I never play well away from home!'

There was not really much that Drake could say, so he just smiled and shook his head. I am sure he was about to have a go at us about losing but Jimmy had killed it. He didn't say another word!

Talking of transfers, in 1962 when Eddie McCreadie was playing left-back, with me as right-back, Spurs offered £300,000 for the pair of us. We just looked at each other and said we didn't want to go; Chelsea was our home, even though that was a fantastic fee them days for defenders!

I often wonder what would have happened if I had moved … maybe no bad injury and more international games. All those are just thoughts and maybes though.

Staying at Chelsea was the correct decision and I never regretted it. The happiness and the enjoyment I got playing for Chelsea, money could not buy. I have never considered money a driving factor. My thinking was, just think how many youngsters dream of playing for their team and here I am, being paid for the pleasure of doing just that.

It was around this time that we had a game at Grimsby and one of the Grimsby players, Phillips, I think was his name, placed a deliberate kick in my creams (for the non-cockneys, bollocks)! As the players stood around me with the physio trying to help, all I heard was one of the lads say, 'Don't worry, he'll get a good massage at the Hinds Head tonight.' Also, Frank Upton told Phillips that when he next comes to The Bridge he better wear a steel jockstrap! Funnily enough, he wasn't in the team for the return match!

# THE WAY THINGS WERE

I DO hear and read a lot now about players and their gambling habits. We gambled as well, not on the same level of course, but Terry Venables and I owned a greyhound.

It was actually great fun; it cost us 30 bob a week to look after it and it was Bob Thompson who trained it for us and he would also tell us when to back him and when not to. We had a laugh. In many ways this started from the early days at the club. I also remember playing in the reserve team and when we had away games and were travelling by coach we would mark the wheel with numbers and then mark an arrow on the bodywork. Everyone put in a few bob and when the bus stopped whoever's number was the closest to the arrow won the pot!

Terry and I had by now become good friends and he was often with my friends and I at the Hinds Head on Saturday nights. One night we took a couple of girls home in the taxi and on arriving at one girl's house we jumped out; the girl I was with lived a bit further down the road and our mates took the taxi home, saying, 'We ain't going to hang around waiting for you two.' So Terry and I arranged to meet at the roundabout just down the road and walk home. With the girls safely home, we were walking along and, sod's law, it started to rain.

Then a police car pulled up. We were asked, 'Where you two going this time of night?' I replied, 'He's off to Beacontree and I'm going to Elm Park.'

'Okay, jump in!'

Now, not a word was spoken, and the policemen did not know who we were. Terry was dropped off at the top of his road and I was dropped off at the flats at about three o'clock, no questions asked. I just said, 'Thank you.' What else could I say? That was London them days and I wonder if those days will ever come back.

It was at the beginning of training for the new season that Docherty also changed the 2-3-5 system and introduced the wing-backs. Usually as a full-back you weren't allowed to cross the halfway line but Tommy and Dave came up with the idea to use attacking full-backs. It was great to be able to express yourself in this open play and it was Terry who said, 'Ken cannot go upfield like that or he will get a bloody nosebleed.' It was a big surprise for our opponents as this was almost unheard of at the time and the following season, we stormed through the second division and quite rightly got promoted back into the first division. We actually added to the attack by overlapping and delivering crosses.

I said before how Tommy and Dave also transformed me. What I meant was I started to really enjoy my football as I was now so much more involved. They introduced more freedom of expression into our game and it was more enjoyable both for us as players as well as for the spectators.

# FOR THE LOVE
# OF THE GAME

I WANT to just say a few words on what I suppose I can call team spirit but this was not just limited to your own team.

There was a great camaraderie with your opposition as well.

The likes of Ron Harris, Norman Hunter and Jackie Charlton were hard men. Their tackles were not light and, yes, they gave it everything. But they would always pick you up and ask if you are okay. 'No hard feelings, mate!' But that's how it was in them days: you were all trying to make a living and you all enjoyed the game. There was a fantastic passion in everything we did and most importantly on the pitch. The players would look after each other on the field and not just verbally.

There was one game at Tottenham. It was always nice playing there as they played good football. Anyway, Ron Harris was playing and his job in the game was to mark 'Chalky', or John White (he actually got struck by lightning playing golf, but that's another story), a hell of a good player.

Ron, as usual, was marking him pretty tight. 'Go past me and I'll break your bloody leg' and things like that being whispered in his ear – with a smile, of course, as he would never actually do that on purpose, but he had his reputation to uphold. It was Dave Mackay playing for Tottenham who said, 'Come on, leave him alone.' Not that Ron took a blind bit of notice. Anyway, Tottenham had a throw-in and Dave, who had a long throw, picked up the ball. So naturally, Chalky starts to move away, at which point Dave shouted, 'Come, come,' beckoning him forward. Chalky got closer and closer and Dave then hurled the ball straight at Chalky, who ducked at the last moment and Ron, being so close, took it full in the face. Down he went, blood pouring from his nose. Dave went across, looked down and said, 'Now effing leave him alone!'

Ron picked himself up, wiped his face and just smiled and shook his head. Now I don't see this as wrong. We were playing football and for Ron he was doing his job and it was his style, right or wrong. He couldn't play any other way and if he'd had to stop he wouldn't have been effective. Dave had made his point but it didn't make a difference to Ron.

This attitude and, I suppose, sportsmanship came from the top. I remember playing in a reserve team game, and the manager was Ron Suart. One of our team made a vicious tackle on an opponent and Ron immediately removed our player from the pitch, not as the referee but just to make a point. We didn't have a substitute, so we finished the game with ten men!

This whole attitude rubbed off in different ways as well. We used to travel up to the home games on the district line and would walk into the grounds with the fans. There was plenty of 'Good luck, lads' and pats on the back. This was one of the best times of my life. There was a fantastic atmosphere connected with the team and even though we had been relegated in the 61/62 season, Docherty had given us a renewed belief in ourselves and this showed in our play.

We were promoted back to the first division the next season and the icing on the cake for me was receiving my England call-up for the '63 tour of Czechoslovakia, East Germany and Switzerland.

# ONE OF MY
# PROUDEST MOMENTS

SIR ALF Ramsey was England's boss at this time and I still recall when he came into the changing room before the game against Czechoslovakia, my first game in an England jersey, sitting there and feeling nervous. Sir Alf came over, sat down next to me and said, 'You would not be here if I didn't think you was good enough.' I believe that standing on the pitch in front of thousands of fans with our national anthem playing was one of the proudest moments of my career. I do remember being close to tears and if I had tried to sing along I would have blubbed, so just kept my mouth shut. It was an incredible experience for a young lad!

One of the best things was when the game started, Bobby Charlton and Bobby Smith kept on passing the ball to me to build my confidence and bring me into the game. I sometimes wonder, exactly how do the international players of today feel?

Another thing that may surprise you is that for your first international games, if you were selected, Chelsea would pay for your family to come along and watch. My first home international game was in the under-23s when we played Yugoslavia in Manchester at Old Trafford. I went up with the team but Tommy came up with my mum and dad, Fred and

Nell as they were known to everyone. Sadly, it was a terrible game. We drew 0-0 and had played on a frozen pitch.

Afterwards, Tommy came up to me and said, 'Ken, our next game on Saturday is at Newcastle, so there is no point you coming all the way back to London. Stay up here and we will see you at the weekend!' I couldn't really refuse, so Tommy organised it all and we made our way up to Newcastle. It was on Friday when the rest of the team arrived at the hotel and it was great. We all knew our team-mates' parents, so for my mum and dad it was a chorus of 'Hello Fred, hello Nell!' They loved it.

Come Friday night, we are all sitting in the dining room of the hotel and choosing our dinner. Dad, God bless him, had never really been anywhere like this where there was waiters and suchlike and I think he was a bit gobsmacked.

Mum, as mothers always do, took it in her stride. Dad had taken one look at all the cutlery laid out in front of him and just shook his head. I had taken a knock midweek and was gonna be rested for the game tomorrow, so Tommy mentioned that I could have a couple of beers this evening.

Dad, who had been on the edge of the conversation, was still looking around when I picked up the menu and started to look through at what they might like.

I looked up at Dad and said, 'How about a prawn cocktail?'

He replied, 'No, no, I don't want anything to drink.'

We laughed, and so did he when I explained.

Coming back to London after the match on the train, Dad was caught out again. We had stayed another night and so it was Sunday when we got on the train. We was sitting in the dining car and had eaten a good lunch, had a few beers and the waiter comes over with the bill. Tommy had arranged it that the waiter gave the bill to my Dad.

Dad took one look and, at the top of his voice, said, 'I ain't bloody paying this. I ain't nothing to do with Chelsea!' At this moment, Tommy appeared amid the laughter from the whole team. Dad saw the funny side of it and shook his head once again with a smile.

That was what made playing the game at this time so good. There was a wonderful camaraderie and we all got on so well. Probably wouldn't happen now but we enjoyed the whole experience of the game and friends and family were always welcome. Tommy was good at that and it showed in our football.

The same thing applied when Bobby Tambling played his first international game away against France in Paris.

The club paid for his parents, but Tommy said if any players wanted to go it was okay, but we had to pay for it ourselves.

A few of us wanted to go, so Chelsea organised the flight and hotel and we paid for those in advance. We arrived in Paris a few hours before kick-off and checked into the hotel, which was next door to the then-famous Blue Girl club; the attraction was it was a topless club. I always shared a room with Terry, so we dropped our bags off and went downstairs for champagne and caviar.

Then it was off to the stadium and after the game we was invited to the club, the topless one that is! It was a great night for all, and we returned to the hotel at 6.30 in the morning, went straight to our room, picked up our bags and went to the airport. We never spent more than ten minutes in the room the whole trip. That, again, was the friendship among our players and a great spirit among us all at the club.

Another good time we had was a few days away when a few of us were sitting at the bar and Terry noticed a couple of girls were looking at Graham Moore. Terry said to Graham,

'Pretend you are a bit deaf,' and he would bring the girls over. As I was sitting next to Graham, I offered my seat to one of them. It did not take long for another chair to be made available. So there was Graham, sitting in between two ladies as they started to talk to him. Graham stared at them with no response and so they then turned to Terry and said, 'He won't talk to us.' It was then that Terry said, 'You will have to talk loud, he is a little deaf.' They did so but still Graham gave no response; the girl was saying, 'My name is Lucy and my friend's name is Judy, what is your name? We like you and would like to talk with you.' Well, Graham was brilliant. He kept a deadpan face all the time, drinking his beer and just looking straight ahead as they got louder and louder. Then, all of a sudden, Graham turned to them and said, 'Hello, ladies, why are you shouting at me?' Lucy then pointed to Terry and as we all started laughing, Graham just smiled, and the two girls really took it well considering they had been duped.

A regular haunt on a Saturday night was the Ilford Palace, a dance hall. It was the usual scene in them days: all the lads at the bar watching the girls dancing together! It was always the last dance that we looked forward to because the lights were low, the music was slow, and we would each select a girl we liked and do the 'creep' as it was called then. We also used to call it the 'slap dance' as while you were smooching there would invariably be a loud slap, which meant one of the lads had put their hands somewhere they shouldn't! Still makes me smile.

# BACK AT THE TOP

ONE OF the club matches that will always stand out was when we won promotion back into the first division. It was at Stamford Bridge against Portsmouth and we had to win. There were more than 70,000 fans there that day and boy, did we give them a show, winning 7-1. At the end of the game the fans poured on to the pitch to celebrate; they wanted to say thanks. A great moment for me and something I had never experienced before. Another very proud and very emotional game.

One of the places I have fond memories of in our training regime was in a small town in Sweden, which I think was called Hindus. There was a training camp we used to go to that was out of town but ideal for the training and cross country runs, with a football pitch and everything. As I said, it was in the country and we had done about three of four days and Tommy said we could go into town but to be back before midnight. We had a few beers and then got a string of taxis to bring us all back, but one player got left behind, you can imagine why! Anyway, we all got back and went to our rooms. The training camp was all ground-floor rooms, so we had agreed to leave this person's window open, so it was easy for him to get in. Just after midnight, Tommy started his room check and we had decided that when he comes into the room to check we keep him talking, to buy time for the last guy to get back. This worked well, so we thought. It was years later though when I was Tommy's assistant at Queens Park Rangers that we got talking about Chelsea and this event came up. Tommy laughed and then went on to say how he knew one of the players climbed in the window. He said he was still fully clothed and sweating like a waterfall but being Tommy, he just turned round and left the room.

# FIRM BUT FAIR

WE WERE up in Blackpool for an end-of-season game at Burnley. It was one of those times when if we had won the last few games we could have won the league. We had just played Manchester City and so, rather than go back to London, we had a few days up in Blackpool. A bit of a break you might say, but as I said, the season was coming to a close, so it was always good when the club made a small gesture like that and we always enjoyed it.

So Tommy had given us free rein for the three nights, and mornings! But the fourth night he had said stay in, get an early night and be fresh for the trip to Burnley. He had let us go out but there was a curfew. We was having a good time, always did actually, especially when the beer flowed.

That was when the guys asked me to phone Tommy and see if they could have an extension. I said 'no' immediately and reminded them they had had three good nights out, they had a game coming up and 'let's be sensible lads!' So, we all went back to the hotel and I went to bed. I half expected them to have a game of cards and maybe another beer in the hotel, which Tommy wasn't against.

The following morning there was a knock at my door. It was Tommy and he was looking really low. I had known him long enough to know something was up. He just said, 'I've sent some of the lads home!'

'What, they forget their boots?' I joked.

'No, they went out again last night after you came back.'

Tommy had sent six of them home and my obvious question was who was gonna replace them. He said he had given instructions for some of the reserves to come up. It was Thursday, so we had a bit of time. What caught us all by surprise though was the backlash from the press for the players and the club alike. How they got to know about it we don't know, probably the doorman at the hotel, but we never found out. Tommy, who was usually great with the press, backed off, so the assumptions flew around, which made it all worse. The perils of beer! We lost the Burnley game and our chance for the title had gone.

It makes me smile when I have caught up with some of those players who got sent home and the few who went on to manage actually put their hands up and said Tommy was right! And then I think of today and what it must be like trying to control a dressing room full of young millionaires!

The best thing about Tommy and Dave was they brought a style of football that was fantastic to play and I am sure a pleasure to watch. We all loved the training even though it was very hard. We could see the benefits of it in the way we played.

One of the things we would also do is to go off to Europe to play friendly games now and again. Quite often, we would go after the Saturday game. Anyways, this one time we went off to Munich. And it was Oktoberfest time! Of course, we got the game over and done with and it was then three days of Oktoberfesting. The whole team really enjoyed it. I mean, three nights in a party town: beer, food, girls and an all-round fun time.

I also remember visiting the Dachau concentration camp along with two journalists. I will never forget the depths of human depravity that I witnessed there, which will be with me to my grave.

Tommy had made me captain for the '63 season and I never in a million years thought it would turn out to be the season it did and that I would receive the injury that eventually ended my playing career.

# DAMN, THAT HURT!

I HAD been selected to play for England against a rest of the world team on a Wednesday night at Highbury in October '63. The Saturday before, while playing against Sheffield Wednesday, I suffered what was called a 'bucket handle tear': I basically ruptured the cartilage and ligaments in my left knee. It wasn't a tackle, as there was actually no one within ten yards of me when it happened. You remember when I talked of one of the ground staff jobs that I used to do, changing the length of the studs? Well, my fault really, as I had the wrong studs in. I had walked on the pitch before the game and felt that long studs would be better. I clearly remember the ball going past me, into no man's land, and I turned to chase but my foot stuck firm and the rest of my body turned.

God, it hurt!

I was carried off, taken to the dressing room and thankfully given an injection. It was bloody painful and I could see from the look on the doctor's face that things were not good. They were trying to straighten my leg and as I leaned forward to push their hands away it was Harry, the physio, who said, 'Oh, so it does hurt, then!' If I had been able to I would have hit him. As it was, they sent me home in a taxi for seven days with my knee still locked in a bent position. On the seventh day I was told to report to The Bridge at 10am to be taken to see a specialist called Mr Frip. Can you imagine that happening today: a Premier League player travelling on crutches on the district line for one and a half hours, then walking along on crutches to The Bridge to see a specialist? Not very professional you may say, but that was the way it was. He examined me and all he said was 'Oh yes, I'll get that done.'

So there I was, in Queen Elizabeth Hospital, I think, in a private room and ready for an operation. Harry was there when they opened my knee up and it was then they saw that the cartilage was ruptured lengthways and was preventing my knee from moving. They removed the cartilage and my knee just slid straight. But that wasn't the solution as there were other complications, which we later found out could have been attended to in the first operation but weren't. It was stitched up and after seven days I was told to be 'on your way'.

I was told to get on with the rehabilitation and exercise but every day I remember saying to Harry, 'It's not right, it's not right,' but he would just say, 'Keep up with the exercise and build the muscle.' I worked and worked but in the end I persuaded them that there was still a problem as basically my knee wouldn't work. I eventually forced them to let me see another specialist.

This time it was Dr Lipman Kessel, a professor and a very highly decorated war surgeon. I remember him well as he had been awarded the Victoria Cross! He was reasonably confident that he could help me out. I was in his clinic for four or five days and I remember the players would come and see me each afternoon. I was lucky as I had a TV, which encouraged more of them to come along if only to watch.

One afternoon, some of the players came to see me as usual and Terry Ven was busting to go to the toilet, so the players said, 'Use Ken's commode.' It was only us in the room so he dropped his trousers and sat on the commode; at that moment one of the players pressed the emergency button and two nurses came charging in! I don't think I have to paint a picture, as we always say. It was the only time we have known Terry to be caught with his trousers down, so to speak!

Terry could take a joke as well as play one. On the way home after training one day, we were travelling on the district line at about four o'clock and were just approaching his station, Barking, when he leant over, kissed me firmly on the lips and said, 'Bye, darling, see you tomorrow.' Well, you can imagine me sitting there with him blowing kisses from the platform, my face was red hot and I was sweating like mad and all the passengers were looking at me. Terry was a classic at pranks like that.

So, still in my hospital bed and it was on that fifth day that Dr Kessel came into the room. I was on the bed, my leg up in the air to help with the fluids and stuff and he said, 'You won't be playing any more. Your career is over!'

I nearly choked and said, 'You don't want to put it any better than that?'

I will never forget his reply: 'Is there any good way of saying it?'

Again though, I'm an obstinate bastard sometimes and I just thought, you're wrong! I would say it's that East End determination again but I tell you I worked my socks off and drove the physio staff mad with my sheer desperation to get back on the pitch.

I would go back and see the specialist regularly but each time he would say, 'You're just gonna make it worse!' I didn't believe him, of course. In all, I was out of the game for just over 18 months and it was hell for me.

Chelsea was a good club and they were loyal to a loyal player. They always renewed my contact at the end of the season. The easy way out would have been to release me but they didn't. They stayed with me and I will always be grateful to them for that. The board of directors were just like the team, loyal to all.

I proved Professor Kessel wrong and did get playing again but I knew I was not up to the standard I was before. At least I was playing though and that was all I cared about.

It was during this 'rehabilitation period' that we had a tour of the West Indies: Barbados, Trinidad, Jamaica and Haiti. We had gone on the tour with the Wolverhampton Wanderers Football Club and were playing some exhibition games. I felt sorry for Wolves though as their manager at the time, Mr Cullis, was very strict with them and it wasn't an end-of-season relax-and-chill time for the guys. For Cullis, professional conduct was important whereas for Tommy, he knew we had worked hard all season, so now was time to let the hair down ... a bit! We had fun but within reason is all I will say. The general rule was always serious for pre-season, enjoy the post-season.

Most times we stayed in the same hotels and we would be sitting around the pool having a few beers and the Wolves boys would be looking down from their balcony and I am sure they were a bit jealous. It was when we arrived in Trinidad, I think, where the plane landed, taxied to a stop and Chelsea went off at the front, Wolves off at the back. We were then met by ground-staff ladies, elegant in their uniforms and taken through to the arrivals area. Anyway, one of the ladies says who would you like to meet tonight? Of course, there was a ripple of lewd suggestions and laughter from the team but what shut the boys up and actually surprised us even more was when the book came out with pictures of ladies to choose from! This was not what you may think – it was purely some company, conversation and a drink. Anyway, I asked Tommy, who said that Wolves would undoubtedly not be allowed so maybe get a couple of girls to come along, no more. This we did and once again, as we sat by the pool chatting with the girls over a glass of beer, the Wolves lads looked on from their balcony.

It was when I arrived in Jamaica that there was a message waiting for me in the hotel. I had forgotten to sign the marriage licence forms before I left, and Pat had sent them out to me via Chelsea to sign immediately. So anyway, the forms were signed but it was a case of how the hell do I get them back to the UK quickly so that Pat can get on with things? That was where the doorman worked wonders for me.

He had said he was off duty in four hours and to meet him in the lobby. This I did and then he took me to the airport, walked me around the back where the crews congregated for their flights, found that evening's British crew and then introduced me! They posted it for me when they arrived back in the UK! Would that be allowed in today's world? I don't think so.

Our last stop was Haiti and when we arrived it was chucking it down; some of the heaviest rain I had ever seen. So as we were driving along we saw people stripping off and washing themselves in the water flooding down the road. Quite an eye-opener to see the poverty that we hadn't experienced before and when we arrived at the Presidential Palace it was almost comical to see buckets all over the place collecting the water leaking through the roof. Our hotel though was not too bad and was up in the hills. I have no idea where Wolves stayed. For us though it was unnerving, to say the least, hearing the voodoo drums from the hills above us during the night! This was after they had told us not to go out at night.

We stayed in the hotel apart from big Frank Upton, who resisted all attempts to stay put and off he went. So there we were about eight in the evening around the pool and in comes Frank, running like bloody hell. All we then heard was shouts of 'Englishman, Englishman, we want to talk!' What Frank didn't see though was that these guys were running after him with guns in their hands. Naturally, he didn't go out again!

One game we had while in Haiti was made a little more interesting with the torrential rain that started soon after kick-off. Well, we had won a penalty and Terry goes up to place the ball and basically the penalty spot is a pool of water, so Terry moves the ball to one side. The ref places it back on the spot, Terry moves away … second time around the ref said, 'Leave it there. Don't move that ball!' Terry was never one to back down and he would always find a way to respond. So, the ball is in the pond and Terry turns around to walk away from the ball for his run up. He doesn't stop until he gets to near the halfway line. He then begins a sprint back to the ball and then toe-punts into the goal! He just smiled at the ref as he walked back.

Tommy believed these trips were all good education of different cultures and suchlike. It was these experiences that I will always thank football for as it would never have happened otherwise and sharing it with the band of brothers that were my team made it all the more special. Would it have the same feeling nowadays considering that so many of the players in each team are from foreign lands, let alone the management?

# SOMETHING TO
# SMILE ABOUT

THINGS HAD honestly been pretty rough with the injury and I don't think I was much fun at home. In one way I felt my one true passion was possibly over but maybe just my stupidity told me I could still succeed. Whatever, there was one person who stood by my side despite her understanding of my injury and Patricia still geed me along and supported me. That was when we decided to get married. It was 4 July 1964 at St Andrews Church in Hornchurch and a very proud moment for me and my family and, not least, my Chelsea team-mates. I didn't really think about marriage before we got engaged. It wasn't like there was a plan, you know: do this, do that, at that age get married, kids, etc. Although it wasn't a spur-of-the-moment thing and we had been together a long time, it still took me by surprise. It was a brilliant day and we had a massive party. Many friends said it was the best wedding they had ever been to!

And then we decided to move house.

I remember when I told Dad that I found a house that we wanted to move to in Worcester Park. Worcester Park was in Surrey and to us cockneys it was the rich part, and he just said, 'No you're not, you're a cockney and you're staying here!' Didn't matter that I wanted to get on the housing ladder. It was a case of 'that's where the rich businessmen live and it's not for you!'

Makes me laugh now but anyway, Mum convinced him it was the right thing to do and Pat was okay with it. We moved to our new home in August 1964 after our honeymoon in Switzerland. The house was originally owned by Chelsea and when I first saw it, Barry Bridges, a Chelsea player, was living in it. He was moving out, I had the opportunity to buy, and the rest is history.

# THE HILL JUST
# GOT STEEPER

I WAS married, living in a new home with our first child on the way and perhaps that put a bit of a spring in my step and things were going well on the pitch. I did get myself back to playing the game I loved, and I even got into the World Cup squad. It was then that we were playing FC Vienna at Stamford Bridge and again, not a player around me and I heard the snap and that was it! Dr Kessel was a regular at my matches and had become an avid supporter. He was at that match and when he came into the dressing room, after he smiled he said, 'I keep telling ya, Ken, I keep telling ya!' There wasn't really much for me to say, especially now I realised that my World Cup dream was over and not least my playing career.

As a final shot they sent me to the RAF Rehabilitation Centre on Epsom Downs. As we all know, it did not work but it showed me something very special: the willingness to help each other. There was me with a bad knee. At the rehab centre there were pilots with no legs, some with one leg, a broken back and a pilot with both collarbones broken.

Well, one morning it was decided by our instructors to go for a walk across the downs. I was okay but as I was walking behind them I lost all my self-pity. There were men here far worse than me, really struggling to keep moving but they did.

The pilot with both collarbones broken was being helped by his friend to smoke; his friend took the cigarette out of his mouth for him then replaced it when needed. And when he wanted to go to the toilet he was there to undo his fly, pull out his ol' man and when he finished, shake it and put it back for him. And there was me with a bad knee ... really makes you think.

As I am sure you can believe, I still wasn't going to give up but the fact remained that too much of my speed and agility had gone, so the chance of a first-team place, let alone international football, was over. It was upsetting to have lost my pace but I still believed I was a good defender because I could dictate. If an opponent had the ball I could dictate where I wanted it to go and where I wanted my team-mates to go just by using the position of my body.

Losing my speed and agility though meant that if I got too close I couldn't catch the opponent as they were too quick.

To survive, I dropped a yard back. Coming back a yard meant I didn't have the same ability and I wasn't the same player – and, honestly, only good enough for the reserves.

My final appearance came against Wiener SC of Austria in an Inter-Cities Fairs Cup tussle in December 1965, but I did not officially retire for a further three years, at the ripe old age of 28!

# THE COIN FINALLY DROPS

IT WAS during this game that the ball was played through, I just moved across to chest it down, and my knee gave way.

Professor Kessel was correct, and my big-time career was over.

Chelsea stood with me though and they gave me another year's contract to basically help the young players in the reserve side. Ron Suart was the reserve team manager then and at least I got a full season under my belt with him.

We were playing away to Leicester one week and our keeper Tommy Hughes received a nasty cut on his chin, so we had to sort out a goalkeeper. Substitute goalkeepers were not allowed then because the rules said only one substitute was permitted. We quite naturally had an outfield player as our substitute. So, up steps Joe Kirkup, who said he would take over in goal. I did not agree with that as Joe was a defender and we would need all the defending players on the field but Joe took over and basically played like a defender with gloves on. He made some good tackles but never used his gloves and we were on the receiving end of a heavy 10-1 defeat.

Ron had very little to say after the game!

I was very proud of all my playing achievements at Chelsea and I knew I had a lot to offer the juniors who were thinking of a football career. I had played 123 games in the Chelsea first team and had never received a booking! Dad said if you foul a player, it shows he is better than you and you must treat the ref like a policeman; you would never swear or curse at a policeman and that's why refs wear black. I never forgot those words!

It was then Chelsea started talking about a coaching career with them, so at the end of the season I joined Frank Blunstone working with the juniors and after just one season with Frank coaching, I learnt a lot and more importantly I thoroughly enjoyed it.

# SOMETHING POSITIVE
# FROM IT ALL

MY SON, Peter, was born on 10 June 1966 and it was a fantastic time for me as a new father. I remember phoning the hospital and they said all is fine and well with both Pat and our son. I phoned my mum and dad and told them the news, and then called Pat's parents. I had also had a couple of Southern Comforts by then and when I put the phone down from her folks I had to phone the hospital back to confirm it was definitely a boy!

Having a son was even more special as my dreams of him being a footballer obviously are there, not that his mother really saw it that way. I joke but I now know how my father felt when he held me in his arms as a young lad. Peter did play for his school team and the local boys' brigade and although he had talent I could see at an early age that he did not have the determination to succeed. Maybe it was hard for him with a famous father but while he was schooling I was retired from the game and was the youth coach, so no glory as such.

Life went on, though. Every day I would go home and pack ice around my knee. Well, actually frozen vegetables purchased at the local supermarket! But the good thing about playing in the reserves was that I was able to help the younger guys come through and after five operations on my knee I was just very grateful to still have my football boots on my feet. But I think this is where the next step up the Chelsea Hill gained momentum. I think having spent so much time with the likes of Mr Ted Drake and Tommy Docherty, my skills with the young guns and my rapport with the whole structure paved the way for me. I kept trying to play on the field until 1967 but by then it was clear that my playing days were over.

# BACK WITH MY OTHER FAMILY: CHELSEA

THEN THE opportunity presented itself and it was Chelsea who gave me it.

Docherty and Sexton were still there, and it was them who suggested I stay at The Bridge and start coaching. Frank Blunstone was the youth manager and I started to work with him. I had actually played professionally with Frank but he had to give up because of injury as well. I actually saw him get injured. He was doing what we called 'long sprints' and I was just behind him and saw his Achilles snap. Not a pretty sight and your heart goes out to any player it happens to. Anyway, I worked with Frank for a bit and Chelsea sent me to coaching school, Lilleshall, it was, and I done well there.

It was shortly after this that Frank got offered a job, at Manchester United, I think it was, and he'd gone up for the interview. On the way back he had a car accident, got seriously injured and he was laid up for about six months.

What was amazing was that the deal he had done with Manchester United was honoured and was kept open for him until he recovered.

To be honest, that's why I've always had a thing for Man United: they do things like that. It worked out for Frank and also worked for me. I was asked to take over the youth team and of course I said yes.

It was late 1967 that I became the official manager and coach for the Chelsea youth team and I remained in that position for ten years, ten very proud years. I actually have a book at home that has pictures of all the Chelsea greats and of the 40 or so from my era at Chelsea most of them came through my youth academy.

The job itself was very time-consuming and so my time wasn't really my own. Tommy had left by this time and Dave Sexton was in charge. I remember Dave was a great help to me. My boys would play on a Saturday morning and I would always go back to The Bridge after the game. Makes me smile now 'cos Dave would say, 'Who played well for you?'; it was never 'How did you get on?'

Dario Gradi also joined at this time as the Chelsea reserve coach. It was hard for him and he was not actually a footballer but he eventually won them over because of his knowledge in the physical and mental aspects of the game. I actually learnt a lot myself from Dario on technique and also his invaluable support of my attitude that the youth players learn from every game and that it's not just about winning!

Dave Sexton always said 'a victory covers a multitude of sins!' It's all about development.

The job was six days a week and maybe too often it was seven! This was not easy for the family. The weekends were not only consumed by youth team games but also trials and suchlike. We constantly had young lads asking to be seen, sometimes with a greater belief in their ability than us, but we had to give them all a try. I couldn't afford to say 'No, I'll leave it' because who knows when you're going to find someone special? It often left me little time at home with my family.

# SOME PROPER FAMILY TIME

MY DAUGHTER, Karen, was born in May 1968 and it was another very special moment for me. I suppose that with all I was going through it was so damn good to have this beautiful little girl in my arms. When Karen was just two months old she was taken dangerously ill but fortunately, the doctors were good and she survived. I would say more about it as it was a hugely stressful time as a parent, but she got better and Pat and I knew we had to be grateful to the man upstairs for all his work.

It was hard work for Pat, though. Not just the two kids to look after but her career was moving on. Monday to Friday for me was coaching all day, and Tuesday and Thursday evenings were for coaching the local schoolboys. I would leave home early and come home late. The kids were always in bed and quite often Pat was as well. I would sometimes fall asleep in the armchair and it was Pat who bought me an earpiece so that when my head dropped forward an alarm would ring. Apparently, long-distance lorry drivers would use them! And I've already said what the weekends were like!

Pat had decided to stop work until both the children went to school and I suppose it was a shame for her to have such a high level of expertise in the medical profession and leave it to bring up a family. I have to be honest and say that my family life definitely took a back seat to my career.

I do remember one summer break when I used the club Dormobile, which I had borrowed from the chief scout Eddie Heath, leaving my car with him, and took the family down to Sandbanks in Dorset. I had rented a large house and my parents as well as Pat's came along. A good time was had by all and to be honest this only reinforced the regret I had not seen more of Mum and Dad and, of course, my own family. To this day I believe my son still thinks I neglected them and the saddest part is he is to a point correct and we don't talk, even now, as much as we should. I wasn't the father figure I had hoped to be, as my father had been to me.

Thanks to Pat, they were brought up well and they definitely knew their manners!

# JUGGLING TWO FAMILIES

IN MY defence, I could say that I had two families and lost sight of which was the most important. My other family was my boys at the youth academy. I was their father figure, their confidant, their shoulder and even after they had moved on to the first team or otherwise I still had visits and contact from them, especially when they had a problem. Honestly, where do you draw the line? My selfish determination didn't help.

This came across in how I ran my youth academy. I had been given the job by Tommy Docherty and Dave Sexton because they knew how I liked to run my ship. The analogy I always make about my job in youth development is centred on a diamond. You cannot create a diamond but you can shape and polish it into a gem, in the same way that some footballers have a natural talent but it is up to me to shape and polish them! I always tried to make my boys understand that the time to be concerned about winning and losing is when they cemented their position as a professional player.

For now, while they were with me I honestly didn't care whether we won or lost. I was more concerned about how they played, how they used their skills, how they played individually and as a team. One problem I had to cope with was the ex-junior first-team players who I had previously worked with coming to me for advice. The rule I had was I only talked technical and not tactical. Tactical was for the manager!

I wasn't afraid to make a point. If someone was not pulling their weight and not playing as they could I would take them off. The rest of the team then had to play a man short. 'Ken, why did you do that?' they would ask, and I would say, 'You've got to learn the right way.' By taking him off I knew what was gonna happen: the rest of the team would have a go at him, and that was far more valuable and actually hurts far more than me saying something!

I had no time for slackers and once they realised this, my family grew. They would respect what I had to say and I remember that I would just walk around the pitch with a notebook in my hand and would write what they done right, what they done right, what they done right! It was hardly ever what they done wrong as I wanted to instil in them a value of 'do what you are good at'. If you are good at dribbling, then do it 'cos God gave you that gift and my job is to help you nurture it and polish it! All about the diamond!

There was one story I remember that summed up the attitude that we had with the Chelsea juniors. It was a Friday afternoon and the juniors were getting everything ready for the game the next day. As some of you may know, the Mitcham ground was on a slope and all day Thursday and all day Friday it had rained. The pitch was flooded from the halfway line to the goal at the bottom of the slope and the goalposts there were under four feet of water. The groundsman wanted to postpone the game but allowed Ted Maybank and Ray Lewington one hour. As their manager, I thought, what the hell can they do? They insisted they could sort it, so I thought, give it a go, boys! They walked to the flooded end of the pitch and marked the posts and then waded through the water, went into the ditch at the end of the ground that was causing all the problem, dived underwater and basically brought out all the sticks and rubbish that was causing the blockage. The water started running freely down the drain and within an hour the water was cleared. That is what I loved about the juniors: I had fantastic people around me, wanting to learn and willing to help. For me, all the juniors had the same attitude and it will always be a wonderful part of my life.

Tony Mariadass, the sports journalist here in Malaysia, summed it up well with the headline on a story he wrote about me in 2014 in the *Malay Mail*: 'Treating players like his sons'.

# WHAT A GREAT
# BUNCH OF LADS

NOW TALKING of diamonds, one of those moments I will never forget is when Ray Wilkins arrived as a 12-year-old for a trial. This was an evening training session and he turned up and I asked him to join a group who were practising heading the ball. I'm sure it would have made a good photo: that dumbfounded look on my face and open-mouthed stare.

He was a natural! I mean, when you're a coach you want to put things right but he didn't do anything wrong! He was the diamond that you just polished. You didn't chip things off here and there, you just polished that gem. Ray was also one of life's good guys as well as a bloody good footballer! It was very sad and a loss to football when he passed away in April 2018.

Every Easter I used to take the lads to a tournament, most often somewhere in Europe. This was all part of their learning about the different styles of football. I like to think that one of the reasons we won the '66 World Cup was because we played our own style of football, namely 'English football'.

Let me say a bit more. In them days it was the most direct style: we was always looking to go forward. Possession is important but that don't always score goals. The desire to push forward, but not at all costs, was a positive way to approach each game. I remember telling this to Ray Wilkins and he quite rightly said, 'But Ken, 50 per cent of the time we lose the ball.' To which I answered, 'But 50 per cent of the time you don't.' 'Play the way you are facing' was another regular phrase that was used. Okay, if you are facing your goal, pass back.

The European game was a great learning curve for the team. The European styles may be more attractive, but I was taught that once I got the ball I would be looking forward and this is what I wanted the lads to understand.

And then there was that time in the early 1970s when the Chelsea Football Club was nearly bankrupt. We had financial people come in and try to sort things out. A lot of that was down to the fact that they were trying to improve the ground and at this time gate receipts were the main source of income for a football club. The players had even offered to take home reduced salaries to help the situation but the club refused. Once again, that was the way it was.

# THE TOP OF
# THE CHELSEA HILL

I HAD gained a wonderful grounding in the art of football but my next move took me a little by surprise. It was 1977 and Eddie McCreadie was manager and the club had just been promoted back to the first division. I don't know what Eddie done wrong but something happened, maybe he made more demands than his ability warranted. Whatever it was, it was the end for him.

News travels fast and a lot of people applied for the job although it never entered my head to even think about it. I was quite happy doing what I was doing because it was successful, not for winning cups and tournaments but for watching the players, my players, going into the first team.

That was my achievement. I would sometimes watch a first team game and think, I've had most of them since they were snotty-nosed kids!

It was during the summer break in 1977 that the chairman had come to the ground and in our usual casual conversation, he said, 'You ever thought of being a manager?'

'Well, I don't really want to leave here, Mr Chairman,' I replied.

'No, no, no, don't leave here, be our manager!'

Blimey, I thought. I told him I would think about it and he just said, 'No problem, come and see me tomorrow. If you want it, it's yours.'

So I went home and spoke to my wife and she said, 'Take it, because now I see you will leave Chelsea as a human being and not in a pine box!'

I would have stayed there for life 'cos that's the way Chelsea were. Even if it ended up as me being groundsman, they were loyal, they were good people. I accepted the job but I suppose the one thing I didn't take into consideration was the difference between being youth manager and first team manager.

As the youth team coach, you are the players' father and you want to make them better. When you are the first-team manager, you are their boss! You have got to change and I found that transition very difficult. Just to be clear, after two years as boss all but Peter Bonetti in my team were lads that I had trained and coached from 12 or 13 years old!

At times like this you really feel lucky to be involved in such a great club. I know times have changed but the club is still the same: always looking to get the best players for the team, and trying to improve The Bridge. All in all, trying to be the best in the world. Mr Brian Mears, the chairman, had the same ambition but the club did not have the finances at the time.

We both flew to what was then Yugoslavia to try to engage Milan Milanovich, who was then one of the best coaches in Europe. I was to be manager and he would be the coach. I was in favour of this as Chelsea was my life and I would do anything to get us to the top of the league again. At the meeting, all seemed okay and Milan returned to London with us to see us play away at Liverpool. We lost the game 3-1 and Liverpool were way ahead of us. Milan's comment to me after the game was 'Your players are far too young and inexperienced to take on teams like this.' He didn't take the job, unfortunately, and returned home. He felt that the club had no money and the only asset was the players on the field who were still young and inexperienced. Me and the chairman knew we had to keep the club going, so we knuckled down with what we had and worked bloody hard.

We just survived in the first division that year. During that summer, we couldn't make any changes to the team and the struggles continued.

This was a difficult time all around, but I did enjoy the job. The advice I would give anyone is never go through the ranks at one club and then take over as manager. Leave your club, learn the trade and then you can return. As far as I'm aware only two people have come all the way from the juniors to arrive at the top seat of their club: John Lyall at West Ham, and myself at Chelsea. John gave 23 years, while I gave 25 – a massive time to give to one club. I do not regret a minute of my time at Chelsea but just wish I could have done a better job.

There are many games I can recall. Liverpool at home in the Cup, a 4-2 victory. A fantastic result for the club, plus a good performance by the players and the football we played that day was excellent, especially the ex-junior players of mine – just wish they could be more consistent. Another game was Bolton at home and a 4-3 victory after being three down with 30 minutes remaining. I introduced Clive Walker, with simple instructions: stay wide and keep attacking the full-back and get in low crosses. This he did with great success and some of the Shed were leaving when we pulled one goal back, then there was a second. Some of the Shed started to come back and by the time we equalised I think the Shed was back to full quota. Then in the final minutes Clive went past the full-back again, and hit in a low cross that was deflected into the goal by a Bolton defender. A great recovery and victory.

And then there was the game with Liverpool at home with a 3-1 scoreline. Some good goals here, but I feel the game was stained by Emlyn Hughes trying to get Bill Garner sent off. There was a bit of a scuffle down by the corner flag, mainly I think it was just verbal. Emlyn then must have said something and Bill turned around and pushed Emlyn in what we would call handbags at ten paces. Emlyn just threw himself down, the referee came over spoke to both of them:

'Let's get on with the game,' he said.

Another was at Man United. Dave Sexton was now their manager and it was always a pleasure to do battle with him. Early on we scored and leading 1-0 from early on was something you dream of. For the rest of the match though we didn't park the bus, we were forced to park the whole bloody garage! Man U threw everything at us apart from the kitchen sink, as the saying goes. And we held on. Dave was brilliant after the match; his words were simply, 'Well done, Ken. Great result for you and the players.' It was a case of instilling in the players that sense of belief that you are good enough and you can show the opposition you are there to give them a game. For the fans, I think at this time they would be praying that we didn't lose rather than hoping we would win!

That was a very difficult job though when I was the manager of the team at White Hart Lane on the day Ossie Ardiles and Ricky Villa played their first game for them. The Spurs fans had created this unbelievable atmosphere that was reminiscent of what we had seen in South American games on the TV; definitely not something we had ever seen in Britain. To be honest, we were defeated before we went on the field! And when Ardiles and Villa played their game, wow!

Their standard was so much better and so far ahead of anything we could offer. I was almost lost for words.

My salary as manager was £16,000 a year and when you think that players today can make that in a day, it does bring a smile to the face.

It was also this year that we sold up in Worcester Park and moved to a nice four-bed house in Cheam Village, at 51 Harefield Avenue. It had a nice garden and it backed on to the rugby club. We'd spent about 13 years in Worcester Park, moving in just after we married and both kids were born there and I think that's why I still have good memories of the place.

# ALL PART OF THE GAME

AS A new face on the managerial block, I remember Mondays was always when the seasoned managers would phone with advice and words of encouragement. They were all good to me just like a junior player needing constructive help. There was Dave Sexton, Brian Clough, Bobby Robson, Tommy Doc, and Malcolm Allison. I really appreciated their willingness to help a first-time manager and when I look back they were all top-grade players in their day, so I imagine they knew how I felt. They had been on this journey through their first managerial post and just wanted to help me.

Of course we all got on very well but after two years when I could see the team not doing so well, I realised the club needed a change. They needed a fresh face and I went to see the chairman.

I had seen him a couple of times before but he would say, 'You're our manager; we like you, we understand you, we support you.' I got on with it but it started to affect me personally. I was not looking at things correctly.

At home I was not myself; with my kids I was not the same and I was so uptight 'cos I wanted to explode. It may sound strange but it was like I was taking it out on my family because I didn't have the strength to take it out on my players.

It was a bloody hard time for my family at home, so this time when I went to see the chairman I had to get it off my chest. The job was affecting me as the lads in my team were my family and I couldn't do the best for them. Well, actually I could: in that I needed to go. My own family at home was suffering because of it and for me, I'd always been a beer drinker but I had now switched to brandy – not good!

I told the chairman, 'This ain't right, I can't take it any longer!'

'No, no,' he said, 'you can do the academy again.'

'I can't do that neither, 'cos the players will come back to me like they always done. "Ken, you see me play, what did I do right? What did I do wrong?"'

I would always look at them and correct them as individuals, I mean, when they was playing for Eddie, they would come back to me on a Monday and ask what I thought! I found that a bit embarrassing.

I'm not saying I didn't enjoy being the Chelsea manager but it's different, very different. You've got to win, whereas being a youth manager I didn't care if we won or lost. My job was to develop them as individuals and players so that they would have the best chance and opportunity to move up in the club.

As the manager I was basically 'too nice' and never in a million years could I change. I couldn't be the bastard I sometimes needed to be!

For my health and my family, I had made up my mind and told the chairman, 'I resign.' I told him I loved this club and I don't want it to be a mess because of me. Chelsea Football Club was bigger than me and the time was right to move on.

My resignation was accepted but the chairman said that he couldn't afford to pay up my contract. I was a bit taken aback that they even offered but it ended up that they continued to pay me monthly until my contract was up. 'Do you want a contract for this?' said the chairman.

I smiled. 'Mr Bryan, I trust you and your word.'

He smiled, we shook hands and they honoured the contract. This was Chelsea and I am pleased to say Mr Abramovich has kept it that way.

They also let me keep the car, a nice 'top-notch' Rover.

This to me says a lot about the club and how it was run.

One of the directors then was Sir Richard Attenborough, although I don't think he was a 'Sir' at that stage. He was well known at that time and I suppose I would call him the classic showbiz type; everyone was 'darling' and a bit dramatic but he was a genuinely good man. I remember one time walking out of the club with Terry and a couple of the guys and Sir Richard appears, says 'Hello, darling', and plants a kiss on my cheek! Terry never let me forget that!

This takes me back to the club; it had good people behind it that made it a good club, very loyal to people, very loyal to its players. You played for them, you played for your country for them, you kept your nose clean and they respected that.

All I will say is that it's very different now and football seems more controlled by commercial business.

After I had left the club, Danny Blanchflower took over.

He had called me shortly after and asked me to come down for a chat. I agreed and came down to a training session.

He came over and said he had heard that the chairman had asked me to train the youth team again but then came straight out with 'I want you to run the academy again.' It was bloody hard to say but I said 'no' and explained that once you leave a place, you leave, and you have to keep moving forward. I don't want to change my mind, turn around and come back. I have done my bit. I have had a great 25 years here. It was now time to move on!

# QPR AND TOMMY

IT WAS about three months later while I was watching TV and the sports news came on headlining that Tommy Docherty had taken over at QPR. I called him up to wish him well and he said, 'What you doing at the moment?'

'Nothing!' I replied.

'Get yourself up here. I have a job for you.'

I first met Tommy when he joined Chelsea as a coach and it was soon after that he brought Dave Sexton in and created a partnership that was gonna change the face of the game.

When he arrived at Chelsea, we didn't really have a coach in the true meaning of the word. We had more of a warm-up and then a game! As I mentioned earlier, we was relegated in his first season but he had stripped out the older members of the team and he kept the remainder together and worked damn hard with us.

I think it was either Spain or Portugal where Tommy visited pre-season to have a look at what and how they were playing. With no surprise he came back and said, 'Lads, we're gonna play a new style of football.' The rest is history, as they say. I always admired Tommy.

Sure enough, within a few days I was the new coach at QPR. I tell you it was fantastic to be back doing what I loved.

Being number two as it were meant that I could always develop the bond and relationship with the team and not be caught up with being their boss!

Tommy's words were 'You be the coach, that's what you're good at. I'll be the manager and take the knocks; you just do the coaching.' I came back to enjoying football again!

Happy days.

It was summer when I went to QPR and there was a pre-season football tour to Nigeria planned, which gave us the perfect opportunity to see the players in action and get to know them. But this was the early 1980s and I will be frank with you, Nigeria was bloody frightening. We arrived safely and got to the hotel, quite a nice place and not far from the beach. We checked in and were sitting quietly when someone started to tell us about where we were and how they had public executions and stuff.

We ended up not sleeping as well as we wanted. I woke up in the morning and over breakfast Tommy said, 'You take 'em training, Ken. I am gonna stay around the hotel.'

Fair enough, he was the boss. I did a short session for the boys as they were still a little frazzled from the flight over and came back to the hotel. I went to my room … and it was empty! I phoned down to reception and probably sounded a bit annoyed but they said to see Mr Docherty. A part of me wanted to smile and think it was just another prank but another part was wondering what trouble Tommy had got himself into. I knocked on his door, he answered and calmly said, 'Hi'.

'What's going on, Tommy?' I asked. 'My room's empty. Where's my stuff?'

'Come in, come in,' he said. 'Your clothes are here. You're gonna sleep in the spare bed.'

I said, 'Hang on, we have our own rooms.' Then it clicked that he had said something or done something and got scared, so I moved in with him. But I never found out what it was!

In the hotel, the staff and everyone were great and I actually quite enjoyed it. It was when we went out that it got a bit frightening. As a rule, for most of us when we travelled, especially abroad, we would phone home to say we had arrived safe and it was left that we would call as often as we could but the wife should only call the hotel in an emergency.

Well, sharing the room with Tommy, the room phone would ring in the middle of the night and the operator would say, 'Your call through to England is connected now, Mr Docherty,' even though Tommy never made that call. You had no choice then but to take the call and pay the bill. An early scam and it was happening all the time. It was not as if you could say 'No, I don't wanna talk to her!'

We went up to the north of the country one day to play a game. There seemed to be people everywhere and it wasn't a stadium. One side of the pitch had changing rooms and seats and then everywhere else there were trees around but hundreds and hundreds of supporters. This was okay but it was towards the end of the game that the police chief came up to me and said to tell my players that when the game ended for them to stay in the centre circle of the pitch.

I obviously asked why but he just raised a hand and said, 'Please.' And when I asked about their clothes and stuff in the changing room he said his officers would deal with that.

So the game ends and we were all in the centre circle and the clothes had been brought over. It was then that the crowd started to move closer. Don't get me wrong, they were not aggressive but it was maybe with the police telling us to stay there it was very intimidating. But they were chanting and genuinely seemed happy as their team had just drawn with an English team. Then a siren went off as the police arrived followed by our coach. It was the police who then laid into the crowd, hitting them out of the way with batons and it was very disturbing to see such unnecessary brutality.

It didn't end there as when we were on the road the outriders ahead of the bus would literally kick cars to move out of the way and even knocking some into a ditch on the side of the road. We then come to a crossing and there was a policeman standing on a podium with his white gloves directing things. One car came to close to him and got a nice dent in the roof. Good grief, I thought, and it was a relief to get back to the airport. To be honest the people were fine, it was the police who took it to another level. I may be wrong and they might have been a 'dangerous' crowd, but we saw nothing other than enthusiasm. It was one of those things that takes a long time to put aside from your thoughts.

At the airport I remember that it was very crowded and I mentioned this to Tommy. 'So many people,' I said, 'and only one plane on the runway.'

'You worry too much,' was the reply.

Now, we had boarding cards but we each had to put some money under the boarding card to pass to the guy at the bottom of the steps up to the plane, otherwise we didn't get on. I was very, very happy to get back to the hotel in Lagos and was really looking forward to getting home to England.

Before we went, we did have a reception with the British ambassador then and it was amusing 'cos when we arrived, apart from the heavy security and vicious-looking dogs inside and outside the house, there were lots of packing boxes. I asked him whether he had just moved in and hadn't unpacked yet. He replied that he was just waiting to go. He wanted to be ready when the whistle went so that he could leave immediately.

We also played another game with a team managed by a Yugoslavian. He told us straight out that he was ready to leave any time and that it was a valuable contract for him, only he hadn't been paid for a while! It was after this match though that another frightening experience occurred. To get into Lagos you had to enter before the midnight curfew.

Thankfully we had some members of the Nigerian Football Association on board the bus as when we stopped at the town border, the armed guards all came on the bus and you do really start to get nervous. It was the Nigerian FA who then took them off the bus, some money exchanged hands, and we got through.

It had been quite an experience and one that I would not forget. And I still believe that those fans were just enthusiastic and grateful that an English team had come to play their team and they had drawn the match. But what do you do? What can you say?

The chairman of QPR then was Mr James Arthur ('Jimmy Boy') Gregory, a lovely guy who always gave it to you straight and who also always liked to have a chat about the game and stuff.

After one of these chats we had left his office and were coming out of the ground with him when outside was a nice new Mercedes.

Tommy, always quick with a comment, said, 'Oh, is that my new car?'

Mr Gregory looked at him and asked, 'Do you promise me that the team will play well on Saturday?'

'They always play well but I can't guarantee a win!' was Tommy's answer.

After Mr Gregory handed him the keys, Tommy asked if I could have his old BMW. Unfortunately, Mr Gregory had sold it, so I left the stadium in my Mini!

Gregory was also the owner of a petrol station, along Roehampton Way. We always called it a garage but anyway there was also a showroom attached as he bought and sold Rolls-Royces. So, one night on the way home he was passing and got his driver to pull in to get some petrol. He got out and wandered over to the showroom. A young lad came out and Mr Gregory told him to just sort the petrol.

Once the petrol was done and paid for, Mr Gregory, being himself, asked about the price of the car in the window.

'I dunno,' came the reply, 'but let me get the key as the information is all on the seat.'

The doors were opened and in he went, had a look around and came out. As he locked up, Mr Gregory shocked the lad by telling him he was fired and to get his stuff together.

'Who do you think you are?' the lad said.

'This is my garage,' Mr Gregory replied. 'I own the lot. With someone like you here I could have lost everything tonight. Get out of here.'

Bear in mind it was gone 11 at night!

The funny thing was that Mr Gregory and his driver stayed at the garage all night to cover things. That's the type of guy he was. He would be there for you hook, line and sinker. But cross him and … well, you know!

He made sure there was money for the club, transfers and suchlike. All he cared about was that the team played well. Sadly, we just missed out on promotion that season.

# TOMMY – ONE OF A KIND

TOMMY, NO matter which club he was at, would always be able to create a good working atmosphere and he always managed to get the balance perfect with regard to being your friend and your manager. I don't think I knew anyone else with his ability in this.

There was one night, a Friday and the eve of a game the following day against Watford that he said he fancied dinner. We ended up going to a Greek restaurant and it was a popular place, so we had to wait for a table. We were sitting in the front and Tommy had ordered his usual tipple of champagne. Tommy kindly paid for the lovely meal and then it was back to my place. Pat had kindly driven for us.

Anyway, when we arrived the babysitter comes out and says there was a phone call for Mr Docherty and asked if he could call back urgently. This he did and basically his wife had gone into labour! 'Ken,' Tommy said, 'you gotta take me to the station.'

Pat had already let the babysitter go, so it was down to me and even though I wasn't keen at the thought of driving after a few glasses of champagne I dropped him off. He got his ticket and said he would call me. I was actually scared driving home what with the alcohol and for good measure it had started to rain. I got home, went to bed and woke up the next morning. Tommy hadn't phoned so I thought the wife was probably still in labour.

We still had a match to play that day, so I just got on with it and made my way to the club. I got there and within a few minutes there was a shout that there was a call for me. Sure enough, it was Tommy. His wife had given birth to a girl, who he would name Grace.

There's a reason he named her Grace though.

'How's everything?' I said.

'All good,' Tommy replied.

'Boy or a girl?'

'A girl.'

'Fantastic, what are you gonna call her?'

'Grace.'

'Why Grace?'

''Cos it was bloody amazing!'

That was Tommy for you. And we won that game against Watford.

Tommy and I had nearly two years together at QPR.

There were many good times at QPR as well as not so good ones and, to be honest, many of the good times were around the chairman, Mr Gregory. Every Friday, Tom and I would go over to Mr Gregory's office in Roehampton for a glass or two of champagne and he loved to chat about football.

We always worked well together, and I suppose Tommy's personality at the end of the day ended our tenure. When I say personality I mean the fact that he invariably spoke his mind, said what he felt when he felt like it.

I did enjoy my time at QPR but to be honest the only time I didn't like it was when we played Chelsea. They all knew me, fans and all, and I was coaching the opposition. A lot of verbal abuse was chucked around, not as bad as you see and hear these days, but still enough to hurt a little considering what we had done for the club.

Our last game together at QPR was against Leyton Orient. It was freezing cold, the pitch was bone-hard, and it ended 0-0. It was a Wednesday night and as usual after the game we went up to the directors' room where we'd have a drink and chat. Our chairman, Mr Gregory, was also there. Now, our chairman was a good man but many people referred to him as a bit of a gangster. Okay, he knew what he wanted and how to get it. I'll say no more except that I got on well with him, I liked him because he spoke his mind. Terry Venables, also a friend of Mr Gregory, was there as well. I was driving that night so I'd only had one beer and made my way home.

It was shortly after I got back home that Mr Gregory called. We were talking about the game and as if it was just a normal part of the conversation, he said, 'I've sacked Tommy.' I didn't know what to say. I knew I couldn't ask why but he just said, 'He can't speak to friends of mine like that.'

To this day I don't know what Tommy said but I did know that Tommy and Terry were not best mates and Terry was close to Mr Gregory. I never asked Tommy what had happened. He would tell me if he wanted to.

The chairman's next words were 'Come and see me in the morning,' and he rung off.

So the next morning bright and early I was in the chairman's office. He repeated that he sacked Tommy and as I knew the friendship he had with Terry, I asked, 'So Terry is gonna take over?'

'Yes,' he said, 'I've asked him to and he seems quite keen.'

He knew that I got on well with Terry and I knew that Terry would be happy to work with me, but I also knew that

Terry had a group of people that would go with him wherever he went. You could say it was a bit like Tommy and his belief in me as an ally and loyal support. Terry's gang were George Graham, Allan Harris and Arnie Warren. Whenever Terry left a management role they were given first refusal to join him where he moved to. The chairman mentioned this and I said 'fair dos', you want the loyalty with you! He ended the conversation with, 'We'll have to wait and see. But you will take the team this Saturday against Blackburn and carry on from there.'

The game against Blackburn was a good result for me as we won 3-1 and the team played well. Mr Gregory's response to the result was, 'I am pleased with you and the result, let's just see what happens!'

It so happened that at the same time this was going on there was also a vacancy to manage Crystal Palace and Terry's gang were in contention for it. The days went by but as it turned out neither George, Allan nor Arnie got the Palace job, so they joined Terry at QPR. So basically I was out of a job!

I had gone in to see the chairman and he said, 'Sorry about this, Ken.'

'No worries,' I replied. 'I've been in football a long time and I know what it's like!'

'About your contract …' he went on.

I laughed. 'Mr Chairman, you're a wheeler-dealer, that's been your life and I know there is no way I can negotiate with you or deal with you. Whatever you've got to say it will be "take it or leave it".'

It was his turn to laugh when he reached into his shirt pocket and passed me a cheque. It was for the full amount outstanding on my contract, paid up in full. He was an honourable man and the only chairman, along with Mr Brian, who I know would act in that way!

We did sign some good players though in our time together at QPR. I remember one player asking for a signing-on fee. Not just a few quid but £25,000, tax-free. We were a bit taken aback but mentioned it to the boss and the phone call came through a few hours later: 'Bring the young lad up.' We did as asked and then the boy was given a suitcase of money.

'Well, what do I do with this money if I haven't paid tax on it?' the player asked.

The chairman's response: 'You asked for it, now get on with it!'

Among the successes we signed were goalkeeper Chris Woods; Steve Wicks, an ex-Chelsea boy; David McCreary from Man United; Tony Currie; and Clive Allen, to name a few.

But the great thing was that the chairman allowed Tom to spend the money and we had a good team. We were only in the second division but we missed out on promotion that season, taking only one point in the last two matches.

The lads were a great bunch to work with, all had good characters and made our job that much more enjoyable.

# THEY WAS GOOD
# TIMES AT QPR

I THINK you could write a good book on the QPR story and I often remember the silly things that used to go on. I was sitting on the team bus on the way back from a game and behind me I could hear a couple of the players talking.

'I'll have that one …'

'Okay, that one's mine.'

It turned out they were betting on which drop of rain would reach the bottom of the window first. They never stopped making me laugh. They all had their own characteristics too. A couple of them always had to go to the bookies before the games and bet on a few horses, another had to have his tipple of whisky before the game, and then one who went into the toilet and had his last cigarette. It was like a ritual and they always performed on the pitch. You wouldn't see this now but how I look at it is in those days it was a sport. Nowadays it's a business.

There were several players at QPR who had good characters, among them Stan Bowles and Don Shanks. We were all very good friends and the two of them would very often go back out to the pitch after training and have their own little penalty competition, against each other. They didn't want a goalkeeper though; each of them would either be kicking or trying to save. It made me laugh though as I asked them one day whether they would be happy to take the penalties in the matches. 'No bloody way, Ken.'

# AND ON TO
# CRYSTAL PALACE

ONCE AGAIN, I was without a job but with the chairman's generosity I was not short of a bob or two. He did approach me one day and said that with the job openings at Crystal Palace there may be an opportunity there for me.

It wasn't long before I joined Crystal Palace as the youth coach. It was a bit of going back to my roots though, as they used the old training ground that Chelsea used to use. It was nice to be back at my old haunt but it was different, with different players from a new environment and there was, how can I put it, a new sense of humour. With so many memories of the old Mitcham training ground, I knew it was going to be hard.

The biggest positive in this move though was that another of my football 'heroes' was the manager, Malcolm Allison. Now he was unique, and I have sometimes called him a genius on the football field. He was always looking at the game and trying to find ways of changing things, much like Tommy and Dave.

For instance, although it was after his time at Crystal Palace when he moved on to Manchester City, the rules then stated that for an indirect free kick the ball must travel its circumference before another player can kick it. Sounds basic enough, but we had an indirect kick once inside the opponent's penalty area. The opposition were lined up on the goal line and our player standing over the ball just flipped it up for another player to volley into the net.

Goal, or no goal? The referee wasn't too sure. The ball had travelled the distance but not rolled the circumference ... so?

The goal was given but the rules had to be amended to make it clear.

Another amusing bending of the rules was with corner kicks. Picture, if you will, a player by the corner flag. He places a foot on the ball, takes it off and then beckons to another player to come and take the corner kick. As the player comes over to take the kick the first player moves into the penalty area, taking the opposition marker with him. The player supposedly going to take the kick says to the linesman as he approaches that the ball has been touched, so gets the nod to just dribble the ball from the corner flag to get closer to the penalty area and cross the ball. I believe this is still the case today. Sometimes it's the little things that make all the difference.

Tommy Docherty, Dave Sexton, Malcolm Allison and even Ron Greenwood, at West Ham in those days, were always on the lookout for ways to use the rules to their advantage. What they were good at and what we as players loved. Think of a free kick and you have six players in the wall. Hang on a minute: with six players in the wall you have nearly a three-to-one advantage with players to attack the goal but, still, the usual thing is to go for the goal directly.

One of the things I would do when training with the Chelsea juniors was focus on the free kicks but tell the lads to go away and think of new ways they could take them. It was quite funny, the things they came up with. One of my players at Chelsea juniors, Teddy Maybank, a good player who eventually had to retire through injury, always wanted to be different. Imagine a free kick eight yards outside the box, the opponents have made the wall and he calls Ray Wilkins and Ray Lewington over, whispers in their ears and they start to laugh. I knew then it was obviously gonna be fairly stupid what he planned to do but whatever, I was gonna let it happen. The honest truth now: Teddy is moving towards the ball as if he is gonna kick it, Ray Lewington is coming up on his right as if to receive the pass. Ray Wilkins meanwhile is just loitering to the left and as Teddy gets close to the ball he trips over but as he is going down he heads the ball, on the ground, across to Ray Wilkins who shoots.

They didn't score but everybody was in fits of laughter and as I told Teddy afterwards, 'You'll get yourself bloody well killed doin' that!'

He said, 'No, they'll all start laughing in the wall.'

I did think about it for a while but never did use that one. I didn't have the nerve to try it in a game. I enjoyed all their ideas though as it was good to see them thinking about the game.

One of the things that happened on a yearly basis at this time was that all the managers and coaching staff would go on a sort of refresher course with the FA up at Lilleshall.

What was amusing was that during the day we would be on the pitches discussing the rules, tactics and suchlike but in the evening I remember many occasions where we would sit around a table and chat openly about ways of doing things, further tactics, etc. The pub nearby in the evenings provided the ideal venue. Even though we were talking with our opponents it was always interesting to get a point of view. I did sometimes call it a bit of a 'jumble sale' because many deals were done at these gatherings, players and staff.

Whether they still do it I don't know.

My time at Crystal Palace was fairly short-lived though.

Maybe I had gone back into the game after QPR too quickly or maybe it was being the youth coach again, I am not sure.

But after a year I was not enjoying my time and felt that I had to move away for a bit. You know what it's like when you start losing the enthusiasm for something, it becomes harder and harder. The game had given me so much but it could just as easily take it away. Even Tommy once said that he had had more clubs than Jack Nicklaus. He was a year or two here, a year or two there but had to change to keep the spark going.

I needed a break and this time I was out of work for quite a while. The worst part was actually going down and signing on the dole. Almost against my principles from how I was brought up but it became a necessity. I hated that.

# SCOUTING AROUND ...

THERE WERE a few opportunities for scouting jobs that came my way and it was Coventry in particular that sent me all over the place looking out for the next great talent. How it worked was that the club would receive reports about certain players and I would get the call: 'Ken, what you doing this weekend?' So off I would go, quite often more than once, and make my report on the player. Other things I did for them would be to prepare a match breakdown on their following game, analysing the opponents, strengths, weaknesses, tactics and stuff. I got a fee for doing it but the good thing was that it kept my mind on the game and didn't take it over.

It was a common thing for managers and coaches who were out of work to do this sort of thing. It got you into the directors' box at the match and kept your face in the minds of potential bosses. If you stayed at home and didn't go out, you would be forgotten very quickly. I would also make sure that the likes of Tommy always had a contact number for me.

Your name would be in the game even if your face wasn't, so you had to be in contact and we didn't have mobile phones!

You never know when a job might turn up.

It was actually my old club, Crystal Palace, and their new manager, Malcolm Allison, who on one occasion needed my help and it was to go up to Wrexham and have a look at a player for him. I spoke to a very good friend of mine, and asked if he fancied a trip up and he was happy to come along. We left at the crack of dawn on the Saturday morning, freezing cold with a biting wind, and we eventually arrived at Wrexham. The icy wind was blowing straight into our faces, so it was bleeding uncomfortable to sit and watch.

For me though, it was very worthwhile to watch a talented young player and we was sitting there watching this player, thinking, or maybe knowing he will do well. I wrote my report and went in to see Malcolm on the Monday morning. My advice to Malcolm was simple: 'Go and buy him! And do it now.' He thought about it and said, 'Okay.' I don't know if they had made an offer or not but they didn't get him. It was Chris Waddle.

It was when I had taken the family for a holiday in Florida that the next offer came through. We hadn't been away as a family for a while and it was good to be all together. Funny thing was the thunderstorms. They were damn loud out there and the lightning, well, you know how I feel about that. I am still scared of it today but in Florida it brought back those memories from the war and I was just glad that they had big cupboards in the villa we stayed in so I could hide!

Anyway, it was six days before I was due to return to England, that I got a call from Tommy about a job. I remember going back into the villa and saying to the wife, 'I got a job when I get back.'

'Great,' she said. 'Where is it?'

'I dunno.'

'Is there a car?'

'I dunno.'

'How much is it?'

'I dunno.'

She shook her head, but I suppose I always trusted Tommy and never thought to ask!

We got back to the UK and I had bought a ten-gallon hat to wear as a joke coming through immigration. Sadly, this didn't materialise. My wife, as usual, phoned her parents as soon as she had arrived, and her mum told her that her father had died while we were away, and so the welcome at the airport was bad news. Pat said then that she was never going away again.

I got back home and called Tommy to let him know the situation. He was obviously understanding and said, 'The job's here when you want it, take your time.'

It wasn't long before I was on my way up to Preston to meet the chairman. Tommy had dealt with the financial side of things. I had a car but the only problem was that I had nowhere to live. Tommy had sorted this though.

# BACK WITH
# TOMMY AT PRESTON

IN 1983 I became the coach and assistant manager at Preston. I was living up there most of the time in a small place called Knutsford, which was where Tommy had found some accommodation for me with a friend of his: a room upstairs in a pub! Best thing about this was that I could never get caught drink-driving. I also learnt to play dominoes.

It was their dog who always annoyed me though, because after an away match I might not be back until the early hours of the morning and that dog could bark. Scared the hell out of me.

There was a good spirit at the club. That was Tommy's magic as he always had that wherever he went. I really enjoyed it and it was good to be back with Tommy but we both left after a year. It had been a tough year and my time at home was limited. How it worked was that every time we had an away game the kit man would drive my car to the match. I was on the bus with the players and after the game I would then drive home and usually arrived after midnight on the Saturday and then left to be back for Monday morning training with the team.

The weather though could sometimes be a problem. That was my life then and I nearly fell asleep at the wheel. Crazy stupid, really. I did get an earpiece though, which would buzz if the head fell forward or sideways.

The directors of the club did ask about me moving up but as Tommy used to say, 'No point moving as we won't be here too long!' It's just how it was. Sad though, as you are always a long way from home. The room I had was functional.

There was a loo down the corridor and the only phone was downstairs. It was lonely. Some evenings I would go off and search for a game to watch just because I didn't want to sit in the room doing nothing. That's how I came to learn the game of dominoes! Just by sitting and chatting with the locals, I gradually got the idea of it but I did learn early on to never play for money.

My weekends were a calamity. If we were playing at home in Preston, I would drive back to Surrey on Friday lunchtime, arriving home at about 6pm and leave on Saturday morning to be at Preston by lunch for the 3pm kick-off. Then it was home again after the match and obviously by then I was really tired. I kept saying to myself what a stupid thing to be doing.

And there was one match, I think it was at Doncaster, and the hotel where we stayed for our pre-match lunch was also the place where Alan Mullery, with Palace or Charlton at that time, was staying prior to his team's game. So we were all together having the pre-match lunch in the hotel and as I was getting the players ready to eat and stuff, Alan and his players arrived.

Tommy was already at the bar with his pre-match tipple of a glass of champagne. 'Come on, Alan,' he said, 'come and have a glass of champagne. Don't worry about them, they'll be alright.' Alan joined him at the bar.

Anyway, we both lost that day and for Alan it meant the sack. ''Cos of your bleeding manager I got the sack,' he told me the following week. That was Tommy though as he had always said, 'We're here to live.' I don't think I ever saw him panic, he just wanted to enjoy life.

That was when I realised that Tommy had begun to lose interest 'cos Preston was one of Tommy's clubs as a player.

He had played well there along with Tom Finney. And that reminds me of the story he used to tell about how you would have a winter wage and a summer wage. You only got one-year contracts in them days and so at the end of the year you would negotiate your new contract. Every player got the same wage in the first team but what you negotiated was your summer salary. Bear in mind this was the late 1960s and early '70s, so Tom Finney had gone in and had sorted a 20-quid-a-week winter and 18-quid-a-week summer salary.

Tommy then followed and was offered 20 quid for the winter but 16 quid for the summer.

So Tommy had turned to the chairman and said, 'Why are you giving Tom 18 and me 16 for the summer?'

'He's a better player than you!'

'Not in the bleeding summer, he ain't!' was Tommy's response.

He still got 16 quid, though!

But Tommy lost a lot of the feeling for football that you need at that level and he had been in it longer than me. I could see the end was coming, so when he did get the sack he said to me, 'What you gonna do?' and I told him that if he wasn't the manager I wasn't gonna hang around. He told me, 'Go home and have a rest.' The chairman was very good about it and paid my severance, not all at once but he was always true to his word and within a couple of weeks it was all sorted.

# CHRISTMAS AT HOME
## ... FOR ONCE

COMING HOME that Christmas after I left Preston was one of the funny stories that has always stayed with me. The company car had to be left and I had to catch a train. I've got my cases and my train ticket but with the snow the trains were few and far between. I ended up standing all the way to London! I had stacked my cases one above the other and just leaned against them for over four hours. Got to London, and then made my way across town to Waterloo to get the train to Cheam. Again, the snow had trashed the schedules but there was a train to Epsom that I knew stopped off at Cheam Village. Bought a ticket and this time it was lovely, hardly a soul on the train. It was 30 minutes or so and the train pulls into Cheam and off I get, suitcases in hand.

As I stepped out of the station the scene has never left my memory. About a foot and a half of untouched snow, a clear star-filled sky and not a car or taxi in sight. Absolute silence and with the dim glow from the streetlights it was the perfect welcome home. I had no choice though and had to walk home. The easiest way was to walk down the middle of the road. It seemed the safest bet as you don't expect any big holes, drains and suchlike. I set off and I remember it was gone midnight.

Just turning down towards my place, I saw this fellow walking towards me. Not another stupid bloke out in the snow at this time, I thought. As we got closer I realised it was my son, come to meet me. I had phoned from Waterloo and it was a welcome relief to have some help with my bags. As I had been back and forth to Preston for a year, it was good to spend Christmas at home with the family but also the fact that I was out of work made it better. Other Christmases I was either training or playing.

Christmas was in some ways never the same after the East End celebrations we had in my younger days. I mean, it wasn't just family then; it was relatives, neighbours and whoever seemed to be around. Everybody was there, knocking on the door, and when it opened, they were greeted with, 'Hello, come in, have a drink.' This time it was just me, the wife and kids and actually was bloody good.

There was a lot of soul-searching going on over that Christmas as well. I'd been living this life, out of a suitcase in many ways, for too long. People would say 'Oh, you're away from your wife, you lucky sod,' but it weren't like that.

It sounds good but it isn't. I missed the kids, I missed my wife. To live like that is not good but Pat's profession and my profession were not designed to work together!

Looking back, it was after I left Chelsea, I was at QPR with Tommy and after that it was just bits and pieces. I had only enjoyed being at one club, QPR, after Chelsea and that was down to the chairman, Mr Gregory, but also Tommy, who was on top of his game as a manager. Any other job I couldn't visualise any security and how long it was gonna last. It was a situation where it was 'I'll give it a go; I think I'll enjoy that.' To be honest, a lot of it I didn't enjoy. I blame Chelsea for a lot of it because you fall in love with a job and then other clubs

... well, your heart and your thoughts having been at Chelsea for 25 years are very hard to sling away.

Basic fact is I could never visualise a long-term stay at any club I went to. I would think, this is good for a year, I got some money for a year. But that's not the right attitude!

I mean, I was on about 1,000 quid a month, which in them days wasn't bad. The attraction was to be working and with the option of that or going on the dole it was an easy choice: to work. The thought of the dole was embarrassing and would always be a definite last resort.

# THE PUB GAME

AFTER PRESTON I had a slight change of career for a short while. I helped run a pub. It was a friend of mine, Tony, who called me up and asked if I wanted to help him run his pub! The pub was just off Fleet Street, in those days the centre of the media world and it was called The Witness Box.

I was at a point where I needed to be doing something, so the decision to work with him was fairly quick and it was a refreshing change, but bloody hard work!

We had a great lunch and evening trade during the week from the barristers and the newspaper guys. The pub closed at the weekend, which allowed me to continue with my scouting work and, as I have said before, keeping my head in the world of football.

I met some great people in the pub trade and I will never forget there were a group of guys from one of the papers who would come down every evening around 6pm. The six of them would order their light and bitters and the usual pub banter would begin. The strange thing was that every hour one of them would go off, returning an hour later and another would then leave, and so on. When I finally got to know them I remember asking them if they had a page-three girl back at the office that they were sharing.

They laughed. 'No, it's the Unions,' they said. 'The Unions say it needs six people to run our press, but we know it only needs one.'

Fair enough, I thought. It was great business for me.

It wasn't long after that Fleet Street started to die and the papers moved down to Wapping, I think.

I was putting on a lot of weight though, as you know what it's like when someone offers you a beer! Even if you are only drinking halves it all adds up. Poor excuse, I know.

There was one other strange couple who used to come in now and again. They would buy a half of bitter and a whisky. The strange part was that they never drank them and would leave the drinks on the table. I was always busy with customers, so I hadn't really taken much notice until Tony, the boss at the pub, mentioned them one day. The couple were from the local weights and measures authorities and they were at the pub to test the beer and spirits. We never had a problem though!

This was nearly a defining moment in my career as I had serious thoughts of finding my own place to run. I had a good grounding from Tony in the pub trade and I was quite enjoying being home every night. When I left The Witness Box it was another couple, Alan and Jean, who joined us in looking around for a pub to take over. We were on the books of a number of breweries in the hope that something would come of it. The best place we saw was actually down in Cornwall: Smuggler's Cove, I think it was called. It was a lovely location but we very soon realised that it would be a summer holiday trade only and that the potential for making a good income from it would not be there.

It was Alan though who said one day that he thought even though we was all good friends, being in each other's pockets all day, every day, in a pub could destroy the friendship we had.

Also, I still think that I was possibly doing this as I was a bit restless, sitting at home and waiting for the phone to ring.

It obviously didn't happen, and my pub days ended there.

'Restless' is the right word for me to use as I was still in love with football but knew that I would never find a club like Chelsea to call my home for 25 years. In some ways I wanted to sit down for a year, take stock and just think about what I should do. Do I keep going from club to club? Maybe I should look for something else.

# CAMBRIDGE UNITED
# FOOTBALL CLUB

AS I mentioned, you had to keep your face in the game just in case. There was no way I could put it completely to one side. I was still doing a bit of scouting and stuff with Coventry and had visited them one day to have an interview for running their academy. It would have meant another commute each day if I wasn't gonna live there, so I said I would think about it.

Anyway, when I got home the wife said that Cambridge United had been on the phone and asked if I could call them back. Considering I had just driven back from Coventry to London I was pretty knackered, but I phoned the club.

I called the chairman, actually, and he said he wanted a meeting with me, tonight. I protested, but he just said, 'It will be beneficial for you to come up this evening.' Fair enough, I thought, and said I would see him in about two hours. After a shower and change, I was off.

At the interview, the job as manager was discussed. He also talked about moving up there but as I told him, the wife probably wouldn't move and I was well used to living on my own at the various jobs around the country. I did think that Pat would consider a move as this side of London was closer to her family, but it wasn't to be. The chairman said he had another interview for the job and asked if I could have dinner with the secretary and then come back later. I told him 'no' and that I was going home.

Next day, I was woken in the morning with the job offer on the table. They wanted me to start 'tomorrow!'

So off I went, and I was in Cambridge the following morning. I ended up sharing a house with the club secretary, which was not ideal but to be honest I hadn't really talked with Pat about a move 'cos I wasn't that sure that I would be there for too long.

It turned out that as I was only an hour and a half on a good day from home in Cheam that I started to commute each day. The job itself was okay and there were a good bunch of players but I couldn't actually buy new players although if it was a free transfer, I was allowed to bring more in.

There was very little interference from the board in the day-to-day running of my team. I even had Martin O'Neill come in for a bit to finish off his career but sadly he got badly injured in one of his early games. I did have to inherit the staff that were already there though and was not able to bring in my own team. But it was a country club and very set in its ways, which made it a bit restrictive. Everyone knew everyone and had a hand in things.

The early starts and late returns home were better for me in some ways as I had some time with the family but my health suffered. It was a good road all the way up there, the A1 and M25, don't get me wrong, so the drive was easy. But I was exhausted.

Coming home one night after an evening game I had just left the motorway towards Cheam and I fell asleep. Maybe it was the man upstairs not being ready for me but I suddenly came to and saw the back of a lorry that I was heading straight into. I slammed on the brakes and stopped but my whole body seemed to shake, and I couldn't move for a few minutes. Seven miles from home and I had nearly killed myself. That's when I said, 'You can't live like this.'

Deep down I was not enjoying the job and I didn't want to cheat the club. The chairman took it very well and said he would keep paying me until they found a new manager. The assistant manager took over and my Cambridge days were over. I was drained and it was strange that it seemed to take the passion for the game out of me for a while.

As seemed to be the usual scenario of my career, this was short-lived.

# THE USA AND THEIR
# EARLY DAYS OF SOCCER

IT WAS late 1985 when I was approached by a guy called
Eddie Mitchell. He phoned me up right out of the blue and
asked what I was doing. I asked who he was, he introduced
himself and then said that he wanted to set up some soccer
schools in Dallas, Texas. This was around the time that *Dallas*
and J.R. Ewing became a big hit on the TV.

'Of course, I am interested,' I said. He was going back across
to Dallas the week after and said that he was setting everything
up, of which most things had been organised.

The main task for me was to put together a team of coaches
and ex-players who would also be keen to come over. It was
quite a good offer for anyone: come over to Dallas for two
weeks, all expenses paid, coach the kids, get some payment
and come home. All our flights were sponsored by British
Caledonian and I organised my side of things and off we went.

We stayed at the Armada Hotel. There was also one car for
every two coaches, so we had transport although driving on
the wrong side of the road took some getting used to. It was
basically babysitting as the talent was not really there at that
time and this was a case of the parents sending the kids off
for summer camp and a kickabout. So the coaches came and

went for their two-week stint, the kids had a week of soccer and this went on for 13 weeks. We had around 200 kids per session and they were paying a hundred bucks a week. It added up to a pretty tidy sum.

I even phoned my wife, Pat, one time and said how good things were going and that she should get the kitchen done!

She did, but I came back with no money. Eddie Mitchell took the lot and disappeared! I never found him and now I just prefer not to look back on it. A lesson learnt but painful as we had spent many thousands on the kitchen, and I was back with no money and no job.

I do have fond memories of those kids though. The smiles and thanks and sheer enjoyment, not to mention the amazing support of the parents. We all said then that it wouldn't be too long before the USA becomes a force to be reckoned with in the world of football. They did start badly as they brought over the big names who were possibly past their sell-by date and one thing I learnt is that the Americans love a victory, possibly more than a big name. Every year they get better and I think it is a strong possibility that they will win the World Cup one day.

# CRYSTAL PALACE OPENS
# THE DOOR AGAIN

NOT LONG after I got back, Alan Mullery took over at Crystal Palace and I called to congratulate him. He asked if I was doing anything and said that he needed someone to help him. He only lived just around the corner from me, so he said to come around and have a chat. Within a few days I was the new coach and number two.

This was the time when I really started to think about what I was doing. Being number two, you are always dependent on whoever is number one. It's a bit like being a boxer and you keep being knocked down, but you get up again and again. Initially at Chelsea it was wrong to appoint me as the manager but that's when I thought to be a number two would have been good and I could progress from there.

Now, when you are number two all the time with the likes of Tommy and Alan in charge, you are not gonna be there long.

You are dependent on the results and the boss: what he does, what he wants to do. It's not really your own life. But saying that, I did prefer it that way. Maybe I just craved a bit more security in my working life.

I was at Palace for about two years and Alan was the boss all the time. We had a chairman there and I am not saying he was wrong, but he put his money in and he wanted his say. I felt that things were happening that I wasn't too keen on and I didn't see eye to eye with the chairman. On several occasions, maybe I should have kept my mouth shut but then Alan came to me one day and asked if I'd had another run-in. 'Yes,' I replied, and then he told me that the chairman had asked him to find someone new. 'No problem, Alan,' was all I could say and to be honest I was a bit relieved.

Alan didn't last much longer at Palace anyway.

# BACK TO WHAT I LOVE

I WAS not out of work for long, as my links with Coventry City Football Club and my friendship with the manager, Jimmy Baron, led to a more permanent scouting and coaching role for the schoolboys as well as scouting for the first team. Not very demanding but a role that I loved.

Their academy was very well equipped and my time was very, very busy again. Weekdays at the academy and weekends either scouting or compiling reports on future matches and stuff. I was happy and I think that the man upstairs had his plans for me and knew that the scouting was something I was good at.

I remember watching a match with Alan one time and he said, 'What's the point, Ken, you are not watching the ball at all.' The thing is that if I am scouting after a defender, for example, I don't care so much what he does with the ball. Yes, his skill is relevant but I also wanna know what he is doing when the ball is at the other end of the pitch. What's his movement off the ball like? How does he interact with the team? If he does something well, a tackle for example, is that because the opponent is bad or that he is good? All these things come into play.

Another thing I got involved with during this period was working with the holiday camps during the summer break.

166

It was basically a road trip around the camps, coaching the kids for an hour or so at each place. I would cover about 200 miles a day and cover three camps and if accommodation was needed I would get a caravan at the camp. I got paid, fed and put up as required so it kept me out there, kept me fit and put a smile on my face.

# THE VETERANS'
# WORLD CUP IN BRAZIL

ONE OF the dads I met at one of the holiday camps mentioned me to a friend who spoke to another friend about me. Shortly after that, I got a call asking if I wanted to represent the UK in the Veterans' World Cup in Brazil. 'Is grass green?' I answered.

I think they actually called it the 'World Cup of Masters'.

They asked if I could help get together some of the other 'veterans' and within a couple of weeks I had Peter Osgood, Peter Bonetti, Joe Corrigan and Norman Hunter, to name a few. When we arrived we had to be checked over by a doctor, being veterans and all. Anyway, the doctor decided that we could not play on consecutive days and advised that there was to be three days between our matches.

Our ten days in Sao Paulo became 30 but we didn't mind.

All the teams stayed in the same hotel and it was a great atmosphere with the old professionals all coming together again in a hell of a tournament with surprisingly big crowds.

One story that sticks in my mind was with the Brazilian, Roberto Rivellino. Now, this man had a left foot that we all joked 'he could write letters with!' After some light training one day, I was sitting with our keeper Joe Corrigan, and we got on to free kicks. My point to him was that when there was a kick, say, 30–40 yards out, the immediate response was to make a wall. Fine, you have a wall, but then the keeper's view and movement were restricted. 'What bothers me, Joe,' I told him, 'is that having the wall pushes you to one side, which makes it even harder to get back over if needed.'

So I said, 'Why have a wall, why not just have the players marking up and you stand in the middle of the goal and have a clear view of everything?' He laughed but thought it might be worth a try. Norman Hunter was the player/manager and when we suggested it to him, he said, 'Ha, give it a go.' Our next match was against Brazil.

Anyway, it wasn't long before they had a free kick about 35 yards out. Big Joe said, 'Ken's set-up lads, no wall.' We took up our positions. Rivellino had stepped up to take the kick and was looking in amazement that there was no jostling to set up a wall and even the ref was looking a bit confused.

We said we was ready, and he whistled for the kick to be taken. I mentioned Rivellino's left foot. Well, it was like a cannon and before we knew it the ball had hit the crossbar and rebounded back out to relative safety.

'Bloody hell, Ken, any more bright ideas? Two inches lower and it would have been in. I didn't see the bloody ball!' said Big Joe as we all laughed. We never did that again.

Things like that though were good and the comradeship with all the players was great. I think it was only the Uruguayans who were a bit unfriendly.

We didn't win the cup but with Brazil, Italy, West Germany, Argentina, Uruguay and the UK all there to play the game they loved, it was a truly great vacation!

# HOME LIFE HITS BACK

NOW BACK in the fold with Coventry, scouting and suchlike, I was living at home. By this stage my son had moved out but my wife and daughter were there even though Pat's working was beginning to look like mine in that she was leaving early and getting home late. As we had both always done though, we supported each other's jobs in whatever way we had to.

Working away from home for so long during my career did take its toll on the relationship with my family. I remember my son saying, 'Dad, you are always everywhere else, up there, down there, wherever, but not at home!' I couldn't argue with him and even though I tried to give them a good life I think I do regret not spending more time with the wife and kids. You miss so much and you can't get it back.

Some of my mates would say 'You lucky sod' in the belief that being away from home was a good thing. It was actually the hardest part for me but football was my life and it's a poor excuse but that's how it was.

In my defence though, there were times when I would have loved having Pat and the kids join me when I was playing or coaching at various places but it was never gonna be possible. I would see other players with their families all together and I do sometimes wonder how things would have been if the wife and kids had followed me around, and not just for me but for them as well.

The bond between my son and I definitely suffered and we, or maybe just me, failed to communicate with each other. Like my brother, he was also a good footballer but like my dad had been with me and my brother there was no pushing him to play the game. If we wanted to play my dad would make sure we had the opportunity but if not, as with my brother, he didn't push it. Sad thing with my brother and with my son is that they did have the ability but not the determination and desire, at all costs, to achieve success.

We are all different, but in my son's defence I knew he was also concerned that following me into the game would have its own difficulties, like the 'son of' label that may follow him around.

At the end of the day though, like my brother, he was a bit lazy and if he couldn't succeed on my name alone he wasn't prepared for the hard work and slog to move ahead.

I respected that was his choice. Maybe I had spoilt him a bit. What with my upbringing and not having two pennies to rub together I didn't want him, as my firstborn, to be going to school and hearing people talk about TVs and stuff so yeh, I spoilt him. But as I know now maybe it was a bit more TLC that he needed! Also, Peter's school friends didn't want to play football, unlike my era when that was all we wanted.

The one bit of bonding we did have was that he taught me to fish and on a Sunday morning when I was around, we would sit by the river with our rods. With six days of my week focused on football it was a lovely break and always good thinking time!

Pat's career had gone from strength to strength and she was a specialist in so many areas that I had trouble keeping up with it: nursing, midwifery, cancer and plastic surgery, to name a few. Mornings I would take Pat to work, come back home, do the housework, do the shopping, tend the garden.

If I had to go off to do a bit of scouting I could. It was a way of life and I didn't have any problem doing it. I would even pick her up at the end of the day!

Thinking back now, I don't think I ever had a normal family life and this was probably the closest I would get to it.

With my career and Pat's career, there was no option. I did the best I could to look after my family and give them the chances I didn't have but I know even that is not a replacement for the bonds I had with my parents as a young kid.

# FATE OR JUST LUCK

IT WAS early 1991 when a guy I had met socially called Cyril, a Charlton supporter but pretty well off, said he wanted to set up soccer schools in the UK. We set one up in Clapham but it was never gonna work as we didn't put enough into it, promotion- and marketing-wise. I remember the day when he called and said things were stopping in Clapham but he had a contact in Singapore that was interested in doing the same over there and would I help him out? Maybe I was in a bit of a rut and this was a break of sorts, the change of scenery I was after.

# SINGAPORE CALLED ...

A FEW weeks later, I landed in Singapore and at this time it was most definitely a culture shock for an East London lad.

I vividly remember a very embarrassing incident. I was walking into a shopping mall and as always when you push the glass door open to go through you always look behind to see if other people are going to enter. Just basic good manners. Well, on this occasion a young lady was coming in, so I stood there and held the door open. That's when she shouted at me. 'I don't need you to hold the door open, I am quite capable of doing it myself. You men are all the same and think we are not capable of doing it ourselves. Well just let it go and I will show you.' I let the door go and, yes, she opened the door herself.

By this time a lot of people were looking across at us and I smile now thinking that with all the noise they probably thought we were together and having an argument. Far from it, though, and I was literally speechless. To think a good gesture could turn into a dispute with a female (by this time I realised she was not a lady, so I have to call her a female).

# AND THEN SO DID
# MALAYSIA ...

WE HAD been in Singapore for a few weeks sorting this stuff out and we got a call from Malaysia. How they got our number I will never know but two days later we were up at the offices of the Football Association of Malaysia (FAM) in Kuala Lumpur. We sat with Dato' Paul and Yap and chatted about what we were doing and stuff.

Our plan was to have a company controlling the training and development. The gentlemen were quite open in that they didn't feel Malaysia was ready for what we had to offer but Yap took me to one side and said that Selangor was interested in doing more on the development side of the game. Would I be interested?

He made the call and the following day we met with Dato' Maslan, who said he wanted to do it and asked when I could get back up to Malaysia to start. I requested a day or two to get my stuff from Singapore first. We shook hands and made our way to the lift to leave. Dato' Maslan followed us out and said, 'By the way, Cyril, we don't want the company, we just want Ken!' Just like that, no beating around the bush.

As we left I remember Cyril just saying, 'Well, that's that then.'

I couldn't say anything except 'Cyril, I have got to give this a go.'

So it was back to Singapore and then I returned to Malaysia for what was gonna be the turning point in my life.

*Back: Me and my brother Terry. Front: Peggy and Gary.*

*The morning after Bonfire Night. I'm on the left, middle row.*

*Me, Gary and friends.*

*The flat where I lived above the bank. Used to be a Tesco.*

*Primary school cricket team.*

*Secondary school football team.*

*Mum and Dad in Hastings on a family holiday.*

*Dad.*

*A get-together on the beach at Hastings after a good midday session.*

*Harry Woods, George Delmonte and I outside George's house in Elm Park.*

*Leaving the house as a 19-year-old.*

*Me, George and Harry.*

*A proud headline.*

The Evening News and Star, Saturday, February 9, 1963

# INSIDE SOCCER

## Shellito Set For Cap

KEN SHELLITO, the brightest of our young right-backs, is short-listed for his first England Under 23 cap on February 27, although he has been out for 18 days through injury. I expect him to be named next Wednesday, the day he resumes full training for his international debut against Scotland at Newcastle.

The 22-year-old Shellito has needed a walking-stick since he twisted his right ankle playing for Chelsea in Malta.

Strong in the tackle and accurate in his distribution, the East Ham-born Shellito, yet another discovery of talent scout **Jimmy Thompson**, hopes to return to League duty against Portsmouth at Stamford Bridge next Saturday.

"Hired" and firing on all four, we hope. Driver Dave Acklin and co-owners, Ken Shellito and Harry Woods, give the thumbs up sign as they set off on another soccer trip.

### All's Fare!

Ken will not lack support from the terraces at St. James Park. Recently he and friends Harry Wood and Dave Acklin bought an old London taxi cab for £50.

So far it has only been used to transport Ken's parents and friends from Hornchurch to Stamford Bridge. But it will be Newcastle first stop for "Old Faithful" on February 27.

*Picking up our taxi.*

*Always a laugh at home.*

*Me at our flat.*

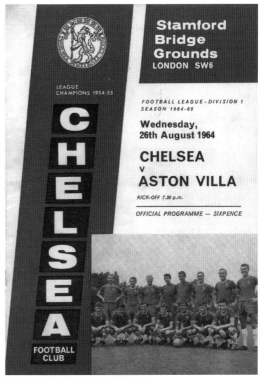

*Matchday programme.*

*One of my very early games in blue – Football League Division One – Chelsea vs Everton, April 1959. © Getty Images*

*Chelsea vs Sheffield Wednesday at Stamford Bridge, October 1963. I still remember everything that day as I was stretchered off, injured.* © Getty Images

*During the match between Chelsea and Leeds United on 6 November on 6 November 1965 at Stamford Bridge.* © Getty Images

*From the left: Peter Bonetti, Mike Harrison, Barry Bridges, Bobby Tambling and me.*

WITH THE COMPLIMENTS OF **Ty·Phoo** LTD., BIRMINGHAM 5
TEA

**CHELSEA F.C.**

Back row, L to R: H. Medhurst (Trainer), Murray, Hinton, Mortimore, Osgood, Barron, Bonetti, Harris, Shellito, McCreadie, Boyle
Front row, L to R: McCalliog, Bridges, Graham, Venables, Houseman, Tambling, Hollins

*Typhoo Tea football postcard.*

**CHELSEA F.C.**

Back row, L to R : McCreadie, A. Harris, Bonetti, Mortimore, R. Harris, Venables

Front row, L to R : Murray, Mulholland, Tambling, Moore, Blunstone, Shellito

*Another Typhoo Tea football postcard.*

SHELLITO . . . plays his
first home game on
Saturday.

*Home début.*

*Just after I was appointed Chelsea manager in 1977.*
© Getty Images

*The press was everywhere.*
*Chelsea Football Club training*
*photocall, 1965.*
© Getty Images

*Me, Bob Reed, George Delmonte and Mick Coles. Photo taken by Harry Woods.*

*With friends at home in a pub in Hornchurch, Essex.*

*Chelsea first team squad at Stamford Bridge in London, August 1963. Back row (left–right): Harry Medhurst (trainer), Ken Shellito, Allan Harris, Eddie McCreadie, Peter Bonetti, John Mortimore, Graham Moore, Marvin Hinton, Ron Harris. Front row (left–right): Bert Murray, Barry Bridges, Bobby Tambling, Dennis Brown, Tommy Harmer, Frank Blunstone, Terry Venables. © Getty Images*

The Chelsea youth squad, circa October 1974. Back row (left–right): Lee Templeman, Francis Cowley, John Sparrow, Steve Wicks, Tommy Langley, John Jacobs, Trevor Aylott, Paul Hammond, Lee Frost, Danny Godwin, Les Briley. Front row (left–right): David Stride, Ray Wilkins, Ray Lewington, Ken Shellito (coach), Clive Walker, John Webberley, Jimmy Scanlon. So proud of these lads. © Getty Images

# SELANGOR FOOTBALL CLUB

MY NEW position was a technical director for the Football Association of Selangor. We sorted the salary and I was put up at the Holiday Inn on the park. Those next few weeks were hard. Things were moving very slowly, and I was just wanting to get things going but it was a case of 'yeh, we are sorting this, sorting that' and to be honest I did question my decision on a number of occasions. I would be in the office early and invariably would go home early; I was bored.

I would speak to my family every day and one evening I was in tears on the phone with Pat saying that I wanted to come home. She said, 'Don't, Malaysia's the only place you can earn money!' She was one hundred per cent correct but sitting there, I was shocked and thought, is that all it was about? Money? Deep down though, I now realised that things would never be the same but at the same time I was very glad that she didn't say 'Okay, darling, come home.'

Fate has a strange way of taking your mind off troubles and within a week things had started to move forward and we had set up a goalkeeping course at Sabak Bernam. I wouldn't have said it was my first choice as goalkeeping is a more specialised skill but it was just great to be on the pitch working with these guys and making a difference. The course was a two-day affair and actually I think that was the extent of my knowledge on goalkeeping – coaching knowledge, that is – but I did have a great support team as an invaluable asset.

There were two other gentlemen who joined me on the organising side of things: Azlan Johor and Ismail Zakaria.

They were honestly a rock for me in those early days and of great support and encouragement. What I hadn't realised then was that they were learning as much from me as I was from them.

This first course attracted just over 100 people and things moved on from there. I was always busy after that.

This was also the time that I was introduced to banana leaf rice. So there I was, sitting at a plastic table on a plastic chair and they brought up the banana leaf, dolloped on some rice and scoops of vegetables, curry and all that. It all smelt lovely but there was no spoon and fork. So being brung up proper, I started to tear the corner off the banana leaf and used that as a scoop. The people sitting opposite me could not believe what they were seeing. My friend leaned across and said to eat with my hands. 'How in God's name do you eat rice with your hands?' I asked. He smiled and tried to show me but got little success. That's when a lady came across with a fork and spoon, much to my appreciation, and that made it so much easier. I am still a great lover of Indian food but I have not mastered eating it with my hands!

# THE FIRST ACADEMY

WE THEN set the academy up and I was working with the players every evening, and I mean it – there wasn't an evening off! We would train at various pitches around Shah Alam and the surrounding areas. Sadly, they have been replaced by condominiums now, another possible reason for the decline in standards of football, but that's another story.

There were some fantastic young kids who came through the academy and to see their passion grow through my coaching was what the game was all about for me. Even more pleasing was that a large number of my lads even went on to play for the national team. I remember one young lad who came along with an earring and long hair. 'You can't have him,' I was told, as 'he looks like a gypsy.' I laughed and said, 'Wait till you see him play.' Sure enough, he was one of those diamonds waiting to be polished.

I won them over and worked at making them understand that the world is full of many types and that with a passion for your talent, whatever it is, things can be good. I am proud that I had the chance to work with so many good people. And that just increased my love for Malaysia as well.

Part of my package did include flights back home to the UK, which I obviously saved for Christmas. I knew Pat was never gonna come over to Malaysia, so it was my chance to catch up with the kids as well. I would arrive back in the UK, get home and be welcomed royally by everyone and then I would find out that Pat was working all the time and only had Christmas and Boxing Day off. I'd flown thousands of miles back and was still doing the housework, gardening and picking her up from work. I got bored very quickly.

Yes, I suppose I was being a bit selfish and my track record with clubs, etc., meant that I hadn't been there as much as I should have been over the years but when I could I made time for the family.

The second time I came back I went to the travel agent and changed my return flight to a week earlier. It was becoming less and less like my home and Malaysia was always welcoming me with open arms.

The writing was on the wall! I can be proud though of what was achieved at Selangor, plus the club were always very supportive of what I was doing.

The work with Selangor had been going for nearly two years and it came as a bit of a shock when at a meeting, they informed me that they wanted to stop spending money on development. My first words were 'This is crazy.' In the previous year they had sacked the first-team coach and despite my protests I had taken over. I had said to them that I would do it until they found a coach and then I would go back to development. It didn't turn out that way. During the close season I had told them I was going back to focus on development and they reluctantly agreed.

From past experience, coaches never last long in Malaysia but the pity is that it can be done. There was one guy, an Australian called Alan Vest, who created, nurtured and built the Sarawak academy and stayed for many years.

To me it's all about creating some consistency and direction and building on the talent you have and not rocking the boat too many times and too many changes don't help one bit.

So, back to the meeting I just mentioned. From my years in the game I knew from the body language of those around the table that it was not good news. I was right and they said they would honour my contract, but it was the final whistle for development at Selangor.

# AND THEN TO
# KUALA LUMPUR FC

I'M A lucky bugger though as it was almost an immediate move to Kuala Lumpur Football Club and coaching their team. Not bad either as we became FA Cup champions the next season when we defeated Sabah in the final at the Merdeka Stadium. We had a good team at Kuala Lumpur and some very talented players to work with but we consistently failed in the Asian Football Confederation (AFC) Cup against other Asian teams.

We did not have the same approach as the other teams and being new 'professional' players, to them it was still a game, and not a profession.

One thing that happened on one away trip to Indonesia for the first leg of an AFC match was the players asked if we could train on the beach. I had no objections as long as there was no soft sand. They replied that the sand was hard and flat so the ball will run okay. On arrival at the beach, I could see the interest in training at the beach was actually due to the bikini-clad Australian ladies who were also there. I didn't mind either, but who will put the coaching cones down?

Strangely enough, I didn't need to ask for volunteers. There were a few ladies sunbathing topless, so I reminded the lads that when they collected the coaching cones, 'make sure you pick up the right thing'.

Our game there was against the army and I had noticed some of the armed forces were wearing one red shoe and one green shoe. Intrigued, I asked one of the players to find out why. When we were talking after the game I asked if he found out. Yes, he said. It's to help them when marching: red, green, red, green, and not left, right, left, right. I just smiled.

Our game was okay but not the victory I was hoping for and you realise it is then you need your assistants to be with you, but that was not to be.

We were lucky at KL and I did enjoy everything: good players, nice training facilities. Not much to complain about, really. On the personal side at the condo where I lived, there were a lot of expats living there, so we formed a Sunday team to play against other local teams. Sunday was always a good day and we would leave the condo at 11 o'clock, get back at about five or six with plenty of liquid refreshment, and then carry on around the pool later. On one game the other team brought a few crates of beer for half-time but I was not keen on that. The game then becomes a farce and a few of the players felt the same as me. If we wanted a Sunday lunchtime drink, we could have stayed around the pool. Sadly, the Sunday football ended soon after that. A shame, really, because I was enjoying it.

It was a bit like the retelling of a story when the club approached me after nearly two years and said they couldn't honour my contract, as it was too expensive. 'That's not good enough,' I told them. After more excuses from them I said I was going to speak with my lawyer. That's what I did and I was advised that they couldn't just end things like that.

There was a year to go on the contract and they were liable to pay up the full amount. The lawyer actually continued by saying, 'And then you can go back to England.' Why he thought I wanted to go back I don't know. I had grown to love Malaysia and I called it my home. No way was I going back to Blighty. It was then that we decided to take it to an employment tribunal.

My lawyer was not allowed in the room at the tribunal so there's me, a judge and the two top bods at KLFC sitting around the table. One of the guys said, 'We don't want Ken to leave but we just can't afford him anymore.' His colleague added, 'Ken has worked hard and done a good job but the money is a problem.'

The judge turned to me. 'What about you, Mr Shellito?'

'I wanna work,' I said.

'They have got to pay you a year's salary,' she continued.

'If they had it they would be paying me, and we wouldn't be here,' I replied.

A bit of a stalemate ensued. Then I cleared my throat.

'Tell you what. You keep paying my salary, the apartment in Shah Alam and the car until I find another job and then we call it quits.'

'You can't do that,' the judge piped up. 'They owe you.'

'Your honour, I want to work here in Malaysia. If they agree with this, I am happy.'

It didn't take long for them to agree and I think they were more than a little bit surprised by my apparent generosity. We shook hands and the deal was done. There was method in my alleged madness though: as soon as they left the tribunal, they would be on the phone to their contacts to find me a job! And sure enough, two weeks later I was installed as the new coach at the Perak Football Club. It pays to be kind sometimes.

# PERAK FOOTBALL CLUB

IT WAS Datuk Seri Raja Ahmad Zainuddin Raja Omar who phoned me shortly after the tribunal and said, 'Ken, will you come up and see me?'

I drove up and we had a 20-minute chat in his office. 'All I want,' he said, 'is someone that's gonna be straight, that's gonna get the team playing football, who will get the job done and hopefully we will win something.'

I told him that the first two were okay but there's no guarantee we would win anything. I hadn't even seen the players yet. To which he said, 'Well, you can bring some more players in.'

Okay, I thought. That was good, in that if I brought players in and it failed, it would be my responsibility. That's what I told Raja Ahmad and within 45 minutes the deal was done. I was to start the day after tomorrow. Accommodation, car and salary were all sorted, even down to making sure the club paid income tax. One of those things you had to have in black and white, 'cos for a foreign player, if your tax weren't paid you couldn't leave the country!

I got back to the flat in KL and packed everything in the car. The following day, I drove up to Ipoh and checked into the hotel. As I knew I would be moving into a flat fairly soon, the

185

car stayed in the car park, fully loaded. I spent the night there and then after signing the contract at the club in the morning, we went to find somewhere for me to live.

The secretary of the club was sorting this for me and he was taking me to places that I was sure he knew I would refuse. This went on for a couple of days, so I found an agent through a local paper. After asking what I wanted and stuff, he said he did have one that fit my needs but that it was on the ground floor, though I was not sure what problem that would be. They had this 'treetop' rule in Ipoh where places couldn't be higher than the treetops, so they were two storeys maximum, usually.

The place was absolutely lovely, owned by a bank manager (at Standard Chartered, I think). A parking space was right outside and very, very comfortable all round. Everything was nice but the price was above the budget I had been given by the Perak Football Club. The owner agreed to lower the rate a bit, and I paid the balance above the budget set so I could move in. It was great to live somewhere that I really felt was 'home'.

Everything was unpacked from the car, but I had to get the car back to KL. Who was going to follow me down to KL and bring me back? Considering I just moved in, I didn't know no one. As luck would have it, a couple of days later, I was having a beer and this Indian lad sat down and started chatting. He asked if I was the new coach and if everything was good. I told him about my problem with the car and he said he could help. So the next day, off we went and, true to his word, he dropped me back. It was a lovely welcome to my new job. And the new car was delivered the following day. All I had to do now was sort out my team!

It was the close season, so I had time to look out for new players and check out the squad I had. Shebby Singh and T. Gopinath Naidu were two of my first signings and even Raja

Ahmad brought some in. I wasn't that bothered with that as he had been in the game as it were for a while and it worked like it did back home. When players were leaving one club they would phone around to other clubs and see what was available. They would call him up and he would always listen. Some were good, others not so good but, whatever, we was building a squad.

We also brought in three Australian players, one of them a goalkeeper who was very good. David Miller was his name and he worked so damn hard. One concern we did have with him though was that he would wear his sweat top next to his skin and the jersey on top of that, making him sweat even more than he should. He was forever drinking water and I remember my assistant, Eddie Glink, saying that this was not good for the body. I put my hands up and said to Eddie, 'This is your stuff, it's medical.' It never stopped Dave working though.

Joe Caleta should have been a better player than he was but I think he got caught up in being a tourist! He enjoyed the freedom of being a tourist and he never let us down on the field but I always felt he could have done a lot better. It is all about dedication and if he had been more so off the field he would have been a better player. There was another fellow, Marshall Soper, but to be honest I couldn't get on with him. Raja Ahmad had signed him and when he arrived and walked on to the pitch that first morning you could see just from how he walked on that he wasn't an idiot.

Problem was he was lazy and another of those caught up in the good times and not so keen to knuckle down and work hard. He was actually a bad influence on Joe Caleta and, you could say, slowed him down. Joe was a nice guy and easily led but it got to the stage that he only played well when Marshall wasn't around! Marshall was only good when he wanted to be.

One practice game we had, there was the two teams and one of the guys was someone Marshall didn't like.

They were on opposing sides and within a few minutes he had gone in for a tackle, completely over the top and unnecessary. I blew the whistle and told Marshall to get off the pitch. There was a bit of a shouting match as he walked off but as he did the players came up to me and said that they didn't trust him going back into the changing rooms with all their stuff there. It appeared that none of them really got on with the guy at all. The captain, Cham, said he would go in there and check. He wasn't scared of anyone.

I was disappointed with Marshall as he had some great skills but, as I said, he was lazy, and he even told me he didn't want to play away games! It was Eddie, who was at the club when I arrived, who told me that he was feigning injury just to get out of training and playing. 'There's nothing wrong with him, he can play!' were common words from Eddie. Problem being you can't say 'you are fit to play' even if we thought it. Marshall was intent on staying in Ipoh and not leaving town. Strange really, and I never understood why.

Sadly, it was something one had to put up with. Remember that Raja Ahmad brought him in, so there was the chance that if he was kicked off Raja Ahmad may lose face.

So many things that in some ways interfered with my game plan but those were things you just had to get on with.

Despite having chats with Marshall on his attitude and stuff, it wasn't gonna change. He was what I called a 'football tourist', one of those players who signs somewhere for a year, a certain place and they think 'I got a year's holiday!' At the end of the contract they are looking for the next tourist spot … and there's a lot of them about! Just look at the number of foreign players outside of Europe.

I don't say I disagree with this but it is a pity when the commitment is not shown to the club they sign for. To be honest they don't really mesh with the team as the local players know that the foreign players are only there for a year. Anyway, by the time the season started we had a pretty good team sorted out and we were ready for kick-off.

At Perak we didn't actually have a training ground with facilities and suchlike, so Eddie did all the medical bits from his house. The house was a bigger one with a couple of spare rooms for this side of his work. We had a pitch obviously at the stadium but sometimes we were not even able to use the dressing rooms. I had insisted we trained in the mornings but coming up to the start of the season we did other physical sessions in the afternoon or evening.

The morning was always tactical as I knew that if we did physical in the mornings they would be tired come the afternoon, particularly with the humidity here in Malaysia. And if they were tired when we did the physical stuff, so be it.

We had to use the local park though for any afternoon training. It was only once in a while that we were at the stadium for that. The amusing bit at the park was the group of ladies who would be there with their cassette player doing their t'ai chi or something. I used to get there early to watch them train. It was interesting to watch all the movements and stuff and I really enjoyed it. I did have an idea to get the players to join them but Eddie soon convinced me that was not a good idea.

So, the first few games began. There were the usual problems as with any team, but they were a great bunch of players to work with. I always enjoyed the Indian players in the squad as well. They would always be the ones asking me to join them for lunch and not with any other motive or request. Just good company and the talk was invariably football!

One lad called M. Nagaraja impressed me no end and he ended up playing in the national team. We found him in a kampung (village) just kicking a ball around. He proved us right in what we saw in him. And he was always such a gentleman, a pleasure to be able to nurture. He also invited me and Eddie back to his home one day and it was literally a concrete caravan. But he was so proud and had even bought us some beer as he knew we liked it. Basically they cared and wanted to do their best and this definitely shone through on the pitch. I think it was a young lad called Lawrence, another Indian kid, who played on the left. Another great player. I also got involved a little in their community and done a lot of work for the Indians in particular. I think that is something that was absolutely vital up in a place like Perak.

# ALWAYS A
# FUNNY OLD GAME

THE FANS were awesome. Win or lose, their support was consistent, even if our play was not. We were mid-table and my style of managing then was to try and keep a team steady and not make too many changes.

Raja Ahmad said one day that I was picking the same team all the time. 'Yeh,' I said, 'but they are doing well.' He just said I should change it around a bit a give them a bit of competition for their places. We had a squad, after all. In many ways he was right but it was my style, my football brain, not to rock the boat too much. If they played good, even if they lost, I wanted to try and keep the stability there and work on the mistakes. But sometimes it came back to the passion for the game and those players that had it or didn't.

I remember one incident while training one day. It started to rain, just a heavy drizzle, but one of the players came up and asked if they could stop because it was raining and pick it up later. I laughed and said, 'So in the next game where it rains I will be substituting you then.'

'No, boss,' the player replied, 'that's not what I meant. Matches are different!'

I just told him to get on with it. You had to put up with things like that but I often think back to when I started in Malaysia when it was predominantly an amateur game. They loved their game and would come straight from work and be eager to train, to work hard. The football was their bonus money, so they had to be their best to get that extra bit, to survive. This changed once it became professional and too many players didn't have that drive to be the best they could be, but that's another story.

Raja Ahmad himself could be awkward and did have a different view of certain things. In a game at Melaka, we drew 1-1 but one of the guys had missed a penalty. Anyway, Raja Ahmad quite often came down to the training area and it was the Monday after the Melaka game that he arrived after we finished. The guys were sitting along the edge of the pitch and Raja Ahmad walked up to the guy who missed the penalty and told him to take off his boots, tie the laces together and put them around his neck. He then told him to run around the pitch. After the rest of the team left, I took him aside. 'What is that gonna achieve?'

'He won't miss another penalty, will he?' Raja Ahmad said.

I shook my head and told him, 'And no one else is ever gonna step up to take a penalty!'

On another occasion we had the bomoh (traditional healer) brigade praying and chanting around the goalmouth.

I was told that it was to prevent the ball going in the net.

What about when we wanna score? Maybe they hadn't thought it through; the result was 0-0.

The funniest was when Raja Ahmad got the team together at a local hotel and some people had been brought in to talk to everyone. Eddie, never being one to just go along with things, nudged me and said he wasn't gonna hang around for any of this. Was I coming with him? We were gone within a few minutes and Raja Ahmad didn't seem too bothered.

On speaking with Shebby later that day, he told us that the guys who had turned up gave the players a football and had them walking around the hotel talking to the ball and saying things like, 'you will make sure every pass goes to a player' and 'shots will go into the net'. What do you do and what do you say to that? It even got to the stage where he brought some of his bomoh acquaintances into the dressing room. From what I heard, as I wasn't there, they would humiliate the players, picking on the weaker ones, calling them cowards and basically ridiculing them. I am just glad I didn't see any of this as I may not have answerable for my reaction.

# ALL ABOUT FITNESS
## ... OR IS IT?

AFTER A year, another face arrived on the scene. It seemed that the easiest excuse for people to come up with for poor performance was fitness. They would never look at it from a technical point of view. So, when you have a board who are thinking like a normal person and not looking a bit deeper into things they come up with the same reason. 'Hey, let's get a fitness coach in' was their inspired decision.

When people talk about fitness, the old days always spring to mind. Back at Chelsea we used to do the bridges run. This was pre-season training and we would run from The Bridge down along the embankment until you came to the third bridge, which you then cross over, and run back to the ground. Only problem was that the senior players never made the third bridge – they crossed back at the second and returned to the training ground. This meant the coach would have a go at us youngsters for taking so long!

Another shortcut was when we trained at Ewell and we would run out of the ground, go as far as the farm, turn round and return.

Naturally, us youngsters would be in front by a long way. It was not a surprise though when the milk float would go past us loaded with senior players waving at us. All in good spirit, of course, and I am always grateful to the senior players, especially Big Pete and Buncher (Bill Robertson). Another very sad day for me when he passed away. Those guys were brilliant with the tips they gave me about my game plus off-the-field activities like drinking and gambling, and I was not the only one they helped.

So back to the inspiration of getting a fitness guy in.

Let me look at things from another point of view: football is not a natural game for Malaysians. Badminton, squash, bowling and hockey, among others, are their natural habitat and sports they can do every day of the week at any time.

Football is an outdoor game, which makes it inherently difficult here in Malaysia with the high humidity and heavy rain. Early mornings and late afternoons become the norm for training and games.

So, there I was with my morning and late afternoon sessions and suddenly the team were wanted for a fitness session from 12 till 2pm! Now, I could look at this as a way for them to gently nudge me out of the set-up as they would surely be aware of my annoyance at this unnecessary interference. This is the way it is here. Don't get me wrong, the people are great, but everyone thinks they are an expert and too often listen to the wrong things.

Miracles don't happen and a team is not gonna suddenly transform. It takes time, commitment and money. The English Premier League proves this point all too well. Problem you get when it's a case of 'let's try this' or 'let's try that' is that they have not done their homework and looked into it.

These things need to be analysed and looked at to see the pros and the cons, not just a headlong jump straight in and then someone has to sweep up the mess afterwards! They do what they want to do, and I feel that is why coaches and players don't always last long in the clubs over here.

One who did prove that theory wrong and who I mentioned earlier was the coach in Sarawak, Alan Vest. He had about ten years there but was allowed to build the team up without too much interference. Alan was building for the future and his management supported him. He left them with a good set-up and a fantastic training ground, which had once just been a flat bit of ground. It had been tailor-made to his instructions. You could say he got their brains in the right place and they were behind all he did. And it worked.

Back to the new fitness coach. He turned up one day and talked about the new training regime. I said no way.

He then went to Raja Ahmad as I knew he would and his words were 'they just aren't fit enough'. I said they were, and then outlined how I didn't believe the three sessions a day would work out.

When I said I wouldn't be involved, the fitness coach said that I didn't need to be there for the fitness training. Did he expect me to hand over my players to someone else? The players would not be happy, either! He was expecting them to finish the morning session, be told that they must be back by 12, and then know that they have a late-afternoon session as well.

He left me no choice, so I said to get on with it. I just did my sessions and managed to put up with it for about a month. The fitness coach then started complaining that he wasn't getting a hundred per cent from the players at his sessions. Surprise, surprise!

One of the last games at Perak was against Pahang away.

It was a bit of a nothing game, meaning that we were both mid-table and it wasn't going to affect things in any major way, win or lose. Don't get me wrong, I always think of the success of the club but a match like this gives you the opportunity to try something, or as in this case, someone new.

I spoke to Raja Ahmad and said I was going to play Khalid. Khalid Jalmos was a great player. Yes, he was young but he was fit and strong and this was the perfect chance for him to get a taste of things to come. Raja Ahmad was at first not sure but he trusted my judgement. So Khalid was on the field. He proved me right, had a good match and it was the start of a great career. Khalid went on to play for Malaysia and in the time I worked with him he always had a wonderful first touch. For a six-footer, that was impressive. Just goes to show that you are never too young.

I remember we played away at Sabah one weekend.

We travelled on the Friday, checked in at the hotel and then Eddie and I went for a walk. We entered a food court and ordered our beer. We were just chatting away when these little kids came up and offered to clean our shoes. They had their box of polish and brushes, so I said okay, took off my right shoe and handed it to him to clean. With that he got up and ran so I jumped up and chased after him. After about 50 metres of dodging in and out of tables I finally caught the little sod, grabbed my shoe back and let him go. Then I walked back to Eddie who was wetting himself, laughing at me, one shoe on, one shoe off chasing this little rascal through the food court. Not sure even now what the kid would do with just the one shoe!

# SABAH CALLED ...

I WAS cooking in my outdoor kitchen one evening at my lovely apartment. It was a tin of curry paste that I mixed with some meat. Bloody lovely, though.

Anyway, on this night the phone rang. It was Datuk (now Datuk Seri Panglima) Anifah Aman, president of the Sabah Football Club. Here we go again, I thought.

'I've got a friend of yours here, Windsor Paul,' said Datuk Anifah.

Windsor had been my assistant at Selangor. He was now working for the Malaysian Football Association on development and was over in Sabah at that time discussing how it works, how it should be structured and all that. I assumed that Datuk Anifah asked him who could actually lead the development and my good mate Windsor replied, 'The best in Malaysia is Ken Shellito!'

Hence, the phone call. They wanted to run a development programme in Sabah and were setting up an academy. The conversation then turned to money. They made me an offer and I accepted.

Later, I had a word with Windsor and explained that I was getting frustrated here in Perak. He just said, 'Heard it on the grapevine, Ken.'

I knew I had things to sort with Raja Ahmad, but I told Windsor that I wouldn't be doing anything without something in writing to confirm the deal. Half an hour later, the fax machine sprung into life and the contract was through. Very professional, I thought.

I called Raja Ahmad. I opened up and told him that with the way things were going, maybe it was better if we parted company. He asked to see me immediately. When I arrived, I explained about the third session that the players were now doing and that it was almost six hours a day of training, which was unheard of in the footballing world.

'But the fitter they are, the better they will play,' Raja Ahmad said.

I shook my head and told him he was basically killing my players. 'They are all tired and that definitely ain't helping their game!'

I then came clean and told him I had been offered another job in Sabah and I would like his permission to leave.

He agreed. I didn't leave immediately as I had a few bits and pieces to tie up but I was on my way after a week.

There were also a lot of people who had been very good to me during my time in Perak and who I knew I would miss. There was a tennis coach who I had met, he invited me round to his place on Chinese New Year. I couldn't believe how many people were there and how much food was on offer. We didn't actually leave the house for more than 24 hours! There were also the Indian lads who were part of the team. They had always been fantastic and they and their families made me so welcome, and fed me so well any time I visited!

Word spread very quickly, and I think it was the team captain who was first to knock on my door. They wanted a big farewell dinner but I am glad that in the end we just went to the local food court. Much better value and a whole lot of fun. Eddie was there and all he could say was, 'Who am I gonna complain at now?' He only lasted another month.

So, it was off to Sabah. It was always somewhere I enjoyed from my previous visits with other teams. There always seemed to be a good atmosphere.

I was picked up at the airport and was dropped off at a lovely apartment.

Harry Baking was the assistant secretary and he took me on the rounds, said all my hellos and then it was off to the supermarket to pick up some food for the fridge.

I always remember when he picked me up the following morning he told me he was a proud Sabahan and on the way to the office, Mount Kinabalu was there in all its glory and it's another memory I won't forget. So he dropped me at the office and that is where I first saw Jeany, sitting at her desk next to the one I was going to use. My temporary car had also arrived, a Perodua Kancil. Harry then said there was a training game on nearby in a place called Tuaran. It was an under-16 game but he thought it might be worth a look as a number of younger players were taking part as well. They gave me directions but didn't mention how far along it was and it was 45 minutes later that I arrived.

That was when I first set eyes on Joey Ryan. I had noticed him on the pitch and I had asked the guy leading the game who he was. He said he was actually an under-14 but he was holding his own against the under-16s. A very talented player and I knew I had found the first candidate for the academy.

Then my next problem began. How the academy was set up is that it was in effect a school in Kota Kinabalu called SMK Likas, and the great thing was that it already had a small hostel attached and, most importantly, a football pitch!

The boys would be doing their studying as well as the football and they would be living in. I wanted to create a team spirit within the academy, so this was my ideal to have them all under my care and control. The school, the hostel and the pitch were there. All we needed were the candidates.

Joey Ryan was gonna be different though as when I spoke with his parents about my plans they were understandably concerned. Joey was their young lad! Their reluctance came from the fact that he was an intelligent boy and he was very used to his current school and doing well academically, so to go from Tuaran down to Kota Kinabalu, to a new school and a new environment – would this have a negative effect?

I was honest with them and said Joey was the first boy I had seen as I had just arrived, and I would like him to join the academy. So, how can we sort this out? Their suggestion was to keep him at his current school and bring him down to KK every evening to train. I wasn't too keen to immediately start this as I needed to see about the others boys that were gonna come and join in and I didn't want to set a precedent.

But I couldn't let this lad out though as he was a great talent, so we would give it a go: him coming down each evening and training.

I hadn't really had time to settle in, what with arriving and then almost immediately going off to Tuaran. So, I was on my way back to KK in my little Kancil, beetling along happily, when seemingly from nowhere this huge lorry flew past me. Luckily this was one part of the road where there was a raised pavement and as I was literally blown to the side it actually stopped me from going over and down the verge.

Back at the office Harry was still there and after a short chat about the game I asked about getting a heavier car.

'No problem, Ken,' he said, 'the four-wheel drive is coming very soon … and you will definitely need that for some for the places you'll be going!' With that sorted, my first day in Sabah was done.

# SOME THINGS ARE
# JUST MEANT TO BE

LITTLE DID I know I had actually set eyes on my future wife on my first day in Kota Kinabalu. Jeany was a Kadazan and as a group they are very tight-knit, and family is everything. We did go out a couple of times but she always had a friend with her! Moral support and a chaperone, I suppose. I was still married and really I think I knew that nothing would happen on that front until I met someone that I really cared about.

Going out with Jeany and her friend was great though as it meant a different topic of conversation and to be honest that was exactly what I needed. I remember phoning Eddie shortly after and telling him that I had someone who came and had a beer with me who was far more enjoyable company than he ever was. He took it in the spirit it was given. Jeany and I ended up sitting at desks next to each other for the first month or so before she went to work with the Football Association of Malaysia in Kuala Lumpur.

The academy itself took up all my time at this stage. Not only did I need the players, I had to get the staff as well and they had to be good and know how I wanted things to work.

We – the management, if you like – had to work as a team first before we started on the players. Datuk Anifah was great in this regard and supported me. It was in those first few weeks that he had organised a big tournament. We had the facility and we used it, bringing teams from all over Sabah to play. I had my guys walking around, observing and taking notes so that we could put together something special. And to think about it, this was a first in Sabah and there was genuine excitement from the potential candidates and an all-round great atmosphere.

There were some that my guys had pointed out but I was not there to please people and if I didn't see the potential, I would say so. At the end of the day it was my responsibility, my academy, and I wanted the best!

From this, we put together some very talented boys and all in all it was a good few days' work. We actually had about 16 players from that tournament. None of them had been told yet, as there was still more scouting to be done. It wasn't long before I had around 30 lads who were then invited down to KK for a final decision. I had originally planned for a squad of 18 players at the academy and this final session was a three-team tournament where we could once again walk around and identify the cream of the crop.

At the end of the day we had 20 players and I remember now sitting in front of them after our tournament and listing those who were successful and those who were not. Yes, there were some sad faces but I told them to keep playing, to keep working and building on what they have learnt. There was always the chance that someone from the squad didn't perform well enough and places could become available.

My academy was a professional outfit, and everyone had to work with me, work hard and earn their place. Just 'cos they have made it this far does not mean it would be easy sailing from then on. I had my standards and for them to succeed in football the hard work had only just begun.

The successful boys received their letters offering them the place at the academy and it was two weeks after that they all came down to KK, parents as well. It was an all-expenses-paid thing for them and they had come from all over Sabah. The parents were down for a few days of R&R and being looked after royally whereas for the boys, they had brought their suitcases with them. They were not going back and would be starting at the academy. The average age of these lads was 13 or 14, so there were always gonna be a lot of tears as the farewells were made. It was important though that we made sure the parents understood what we were doing and how their boys fitted in. They needed the peace of mind.

To begin with, we allowed them to pop home for a few days once every six weeks but I soon realised that at this age it needed to be more often, so we changed it to every four weeks. I mean, these boys have brothers, sisters and extended family as well as their parents to miss.

The boys were a good bunch and it actually surprised me that we never had no trouble at the hostel. There were no bullies, no one making things difficult, which made me pretty proud. The one thing that did occur though was one of the lads who was slowly getting worse and worse as a player. I realised early on that it was the fact that he missed home and it wasn't long before I arranged for him to leave the hostel and spend time with his family. The plan was for him to come to training every night but it went from the five nights down to four, then three and in the end I had to let him go. I would always keep an eye on him for the future but for now he just was not ready. Whether it was family pressure as well, who knows, but the fact remains it wasn't gonna work for the academy.

Joey Ryan on the other hand never missed a training session despite living at home. I really admire his folks in that they really supported me as well as Joey and kept to their word with the training. Joey though quietly said to me one day that he did want to stay full-time at the academy.

It was not long after that he had his exams at his school in Tuaran and did very well. It was the right time for him to speak to his parents about moving to the academy, and they agreed.

My assistant at the academy was a guy called Azah Ezrein. A chip off the old block, you could say, as he had that desire and drive and was able to motivate the boys and keep their passion alive and I never had any problem relying on him to do what I needed. The academy was doing well and it makes me laugh now how some of the training methods I introduced were looked on as crazy. I tried to give the boys match practice as much as possible and we often played other local schools.

There was one game where before the kick-off I spoke with my goalie. He was a tall lad, not so proficient in English, but he worked hard. Anyway, I told him he was not allowed to kick the ball from his hands. When he picked the ball up he could only throw it to one of his team-mates and he could only throw it underarm! Part of my training at the academy was about building from the back and trying to get it through to them that if the goalie just kicks it every time, then about 80 per cent of these will go straight to the opposition and you lose any momentum. I said I wanted them to do what we had been practising. He threw it out and then we passed it, passed it and moved forward as a unit. And now look at those top teams that all build from the back! One of the best compliments for me was when parents from both teams said, 'Don't they pass the ball well!' They got used to my crazy ideas, as they called them, but there was definitely method in my madness.

From my experience back in the UK, there were always times when an opposing team might get frustrated by a style of play and actually become aggressive. I told the boys it was always important not to humiliate your opposition. Pass the ball around, keep the ball but always move forward. You are not just keeping the ball to keep it from the opposition, you still wanna score in their net, so play the game.

The main aim of the academy was to prepare these kids for playing in the state teams as they progressed and we were successful in this with many of them moving up through the ranks and playing their game at state level. The squad had worked hard, and we were together for a few years with many of them, as I said, ready to take a step out of the academy and into the state set-up.

One of the things that happened on a fairly regular basis were the tournaments and one of these was at the Police Academy fields in KL. It had been organised by the FAM and every state was represented there. In one of the games, we was playing Kelantan and I am fairly sure it was my U-13 boys but anyway, I said to Azah that I was gonna go around to the other side of the field to talk with my left-back.

He was a young lad who was always keen and always learning. I wanted to talk to him about his positioning when he was not on the ball, e.g., if the ball was upfield or on the left side, etc. I didn't want him just gazing at the trees! As I said, he was a good learner and as the game went on he understood more and more and he was enjoying himself.

At half-time I came back to the bench and the referee wanders over. 'There's been a complaint, Ken,' he said.

'Kelantan have said they are not happy with you coaching from the other side of the field!'

'I am not coaching,' I replied, 'just telling the boy about his positioning, you know: push up, push back, push across. Educating him on how to play as a left-back.'

'Can't you do that from the bench?'

'Not ideal. It's better to be able to speak to him and not shout across the field.' Even the linesman agreed with me.

'How about for the second half you just stay on the bench?' the referee suggested.

'Okay,' I answered, knowing that my left-back was gonna be right in front of me when they swapped ends for the second half.

*1965 Chelsea team photograph (signed), courtesy of Stewart Willoughby.*

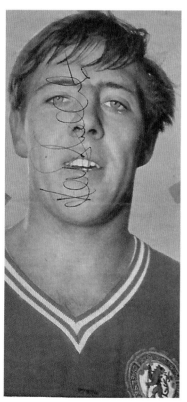

*I might have been a pin-up in today's game (thank you, Stewart Willoughby).*

*Great press for the juniors and a great moment for me.*

*My testimonial programme, courtesy of Chelsea Football Club (thank you, Alan Young, for the scan).*

*That really hurt.*

*Ron Suart and I before a training game in Sweden, May 1978.*
*© Ove Martin Fjellhoy.*

*Coaching the Perak team.*

*Me working at the AFC.*

*Hasan Al Sabah, John Terry and myself during a Chelsea trip to the AFC House.*

*Me and Tom Docherty.*

*Me and brother
Terry with Mum.*

*Me and my mum.*

*Jeany
and my mum.*

*Dave Acklin, me, Harry Woods and George Delmonte.*

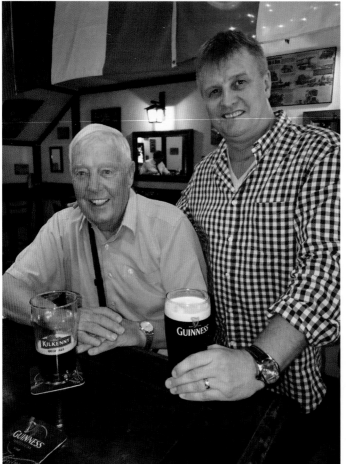

*Me and Nick Atkinson having a celebratory pint after signing the deal with MPH Group Publishing.*

*Nagaraja, his mum, his brother, and me. One of my great players in Ipoh.*

*Eddie Glink, me and two ladies who ran the bar we frequented.*

*The local stadium.*

*My visit to an academy in Cambodia.*

*Presenting prizes at a tournament – great motivation for the kids.*

*The wooden house at Chelsea Hill, looking better.*

*Wooden house, finished.*

*My brother-in-law Joe.*

*Brother-in-law Ken, Denny, Ali, me and Danny Boy in the kampung.*

*Our bungalow on Chelsea Hill, finished – my paradise.*

*Chelsea Hill.*

*My daughter Karen, my granddaughter Lara, my wife Jeany, and son-in-law John.*

*With my granddaughter Lara on our trip to the coast.*

*Jeany and I in our traditional Kadazan costumes.*

*Jeany and I on holiday.*

*September 2018 – with my good friend Bojan Hodak and his son Luka, who I am sure will be a name to look out for in the future.*

*My wife Jeany's family.*

*Me and Jeany.*

*My princess, Kenya.*

*The family portrait.*

*Ken Shellito's ashes were interred at Stamford Bridge on 9 August 2019.*
Pictures courtesy Ian Swoish

# NOT JUST ABOUT WINNING

AFTER THE game, the Kelantan manager came up and said he was sorry about his complaint.

'No, you're not,' I replied. 'You only come here to win. I wanna make sure my boys are trained as well.'

'Of course we are here to win,' he said. 'That's what it's all about.'

I shook my head and told him, 'I am here to educate my boys on playing football. If every team did the same, what a wonderful set-up that would be and our improvement would be tremendous. You come here, just kick the ball forward, chase it and try to score! That is not gonna create footballers. I'd like to see your training session. What do you do in training?'

'We do a lot of passing and dribbling and ball skills,' the manager said.

'So why not do that in the bleeding game?' was all I could say.

I bumped into the manager several months later and they had come around to my way of thinking. When there is too much emphasis put on winning, especially when training U-13 and U-14 teams, it actually kills football.

Winning covers a multitude of sins, but as Dave Sexton used to say to me, 'It's not just about winning, with development it's about learning and improving!' I think that is one of the problems they now have in Malaysia in that there is not enough learning involved and, yes, they may win a tournament but that does not always mean the team is improving. If you are coaching young children, you need to show them how to do things and how it helps their game.

Of course you have those that pick it up quicker than others, like any discipline in their education. I will say though that we don't make a footballer. That is from the man upstairs. We just polish the diamond!

I have often been asked what makes a footballer. I would love to know but think about it: you don't get many university-educated footballers. They have spent their time studying and getting the grades. If, like me, they didn't focus at school but instead had a determination to 'be a footballer', what more can I say?

# FEEDING THE TALENT

NURTURING THE talent is obviously a vital element, which reminds me of the game I was watching one time when I was travelling around Sabah to see what talent there was and to bring it to the academy. There was a little lad, I think he may have been under 11, but he was skilful, had good balance and was confident. He had picked the ball up and had dribbled across the pitch, passed a couple of players but then got caught, lost the ball and the opposition went on to score. The teacher on the touchline went mad, shouted at him and took him off. The young lad walked off in tears.

Half-time came, and after the teacher had finished I went up to him. Apparently, he yelled at the young lad for losing the ball. Was that all? 'Well, he won't dribble the ball again!' the teacher continued.

I told him he had a bigger problem than that: he won't play football again. 'You've destroyed his confidence and embarrassed him,' I went on. 'You could have so easily just said to him that he had done good but dribbling across the pitch was not the best thing to do; he should attack his opponent's goal when dribbling, always go forward and be positive and most important, to learn from his mistakes.'

Again, it was that focus on winning at all costs!

# YES COACH

RON SMITH was still the state coach and I had a lot of time for him. I honestly believe at the time he was one of the best coaches in Malaysia. From England originally, he had emigrated to Australia and fine-tuned his coaching skills there before coming to Malaysia.

Well, I had come in one morning and there was a blazing row going on in the main office. One of the committee members then came out and just said I was gonna be the new state coach.

'No, I ain't,' I replied, 'you got a good one already!'

To which he said, 'He's making too many demands!'

I didn't say any more and just walked out of the office as there was no way that I wanted anyone else coming out and saying, 'Ken, I wanna have a word.' I made it quite obvious that I did not wanna do that job! I knew I would have to take them on for a bit but trying to combine both the academy and the first team was gonna be tough.

I was also having my own personal issues as well. The loneliness was one of these that came and went. Quite often, a haunt of mine was the beach up at Tanjung Aru. Okay, there is the big Shangri-La there now but back then it was just tin huts on the beach. And there was this little Chinese lady who was one of the few who sold beer and who made a lovely mee goreng. I was a regular a few evenings a week and she usually had the beer waiting for me at 6.30, nice and cold! I would sit there and do the programme for the following day. I still remember the view and it inspired me in many ways.

On returning to the apartment though, I would look around and, well, nothing new, nothing different. It was lonely, and I mean really lonely. I would get up in the morning and it's off to training. This was with the first team as I was doing the two jobs then and it would be the academy in the afternoon.

That kept me and my enthusiasm going and I enjoyed that. But deep down, and being realistic, I knew that both were suffering because of this.

I sat with Datuk Anifah one day and explained this and that we needed a coach for the first team to keep the effort focused. He took it well and said, 'Well, Ken, if that's what you want. Find me one!'

Bleeding hell, I thought, what have I done? What a big mouth I've got. So I had to find him a coach for the first team!

By chance, one of the groups of people I had been in touch with out this way was the coach at Brunei. I have said how the grapevine works, and I knew he was looking to get out of Brunei and was looking for opportunities. I did have to think long and hard though as I knew him as a person but not as a coach. He had been in Brunei for a couple of years so I realised he must have something and put it to him one evening. I told him I could appoint him but could not deal with the money side of things. There were committees and stuff for all that. He was okay with it and I asked him to get over to Sabah. A few days later I picked him up from the airport. He was an ex-Wolves player named David Woodfield.

In the end he accepted the job and I thought I could get my focus back on the academy.

It was only a month later that I got a call from Anifah asking me to go along to the first-team training. Though I had the academy stuff to do, he insisted and asked me to get Azah to take over for the day. When I got there, I realised why Anifah wanted me to have a look: David was a disaster. He was giving the team training that was for kids. Don't get me wrong, they need technical practice, but they won't accept it.

Learning how to pass the ball was for the kids! The players had complained to Anifah and I had to speak to David to ask him to upgrade the training – more tactical, more physical work and stuff like that. He quite rightly said they weren't ready for it. I knew they weren't, I told him, 'but doing it your way, you won't be here for long.'

The message was clear, and I told him that even if it was me training them they wouldn't like it. It was the way it was and getting down to basics. Players don't accept being told they don't have the technical skill. Players wanna win games: how they win it, and they wanna win it instantly, as opposed to six months down the road after working hard. The players think they can do it and they wanna get their bonuses and if you tell them different they will feel insulted and then it is doubly hard to get them working with you again. I think it's called politics! I told David to 'play the game' but the damage was done and even though he stayed on for a while, it was never gonna be right between him and the players.

I had a call from one of the committee members shortly after this all blew up and he asked me what I was doing this coming Saturday. It was my day off as the academy was closed for the kids to spend the weekend at home. The committee member wanted me to go to Johor to basically tell David he was going to be sacked. I felt it was maybe right that he heard it from me. David took it as well as I expected. I think he knew his days were numbered.

But who was gonna take the team? It was decided that the assistant coach would have the honours as I didn't know what David had been doing with the guys, so it was better for his assistant. It was funny when I told him though as the colour just drained from his face. I think he fully understood what the team were like!

David stayed on in Sabah for a while though as he was a qualified teacher and he picked up another job quite quickly. I continued with the kids, but it was only a few weeks along when Datuk Anifah pulled me aside and asked me to take the first team for their upcoming match against Kuala Lumpur.

He then went on to say that an old acquaintance, Ken Worden, was coming along to take a look at possibly taking over. Worden was the ex-coach of Selangor and I had no problem with it apart from knowing that he had a bad mouth on him!

I was happy with it though as it would free up my time for the academy. The week before, on the Wednesday evening, I had got home from training and was just settling at home when the phone rang. It was two of the committee members, who 'were just passing your place and thought we would say hello.'

Yeh, right, I thought. I laughed and just told them to come on in. Within five minutes they were in my living room.

They just stood there and were stumbling over their words so I helped them out. 'Worden's coming to the game at the weekend and you want him to sit on the bench, right?'

They seemed surprised. 'How did you know?'

'This is football guys, I know how it works. Anyway, I am fine with that. I will go and sit in the stands. Don't worry about it.'

They left and I thought about whether or not he would do the job well. I wanted him to be successful as it freed me up for the kids.

My other concern was the effort I had put into selecting the team for the game and in particular one young lad, Ryatuddin, a left centre-back who had this uncanny ability: whenever the ball came over from a cross or corner, he was always the one to clear the line and it was his head that met it. A lucky player or a brilliant player, I would ask. Well, I announced the team and selected Ryatuddin for his first game for Sabah. I saw his shock from the look on his face but I took him aside and told him exactly what Sir Alf Ramsey told me before my first England start: 'If you wasn't good enough I wouldn't have selected you!'

So the game took place, I was in the stands and Worden was on the bench. It was a good game, Ryatuddin had a good one too, and we won 2-1. Back in the changing room after the match, I congratulated the lads and they all came forward and patted me on the back. Worden was almost pushed into the background and a part of me thought that I shouldn't have gone in there, even though I had selected and coached the team, it was his to savour for the moment.

Knowing his character, you could say he was a bit selfish and liked to put himself first. Anyway, I had gone in and there was nothing I could do about it now. I left the lads to enjoy the win and didn't even talk to the press about the game. No, I thought, this is one for Worden.

Maybe I should have said a few words as reading the papers the following morning I was disappointed to say the least. Worden had said, 'We was better in the second half 'cos I made a few adjustments and moved the players around 'cos they was in the wrong position.' He never done no such thing. I was at the bleeding match, so I know exactly what did and didn't happen. To say what he said was having a dig at me and I didn't like that. But that is the sort of character he was and I have to say sometimes he had an overinflated opinion of his gift to football.

So Ken Worden was the new guy in charge of the first team and I had my focus back on the academy. I am not sure whether I was surprised or not, but it was not long after that Datuk Anifah called me and said to pop in and see him.

When I arrived, he said, 'Ken, can you come along to training and have a look for me?' Here we go again, I thought, but for different reasons to Woodfield. Datuk Anifah had received complaints from the players, but more to do with Worden's verbal abuse and comments while training. No surprise there.

I went to the next session and his training was fine. It was just his mouth and how he spoke to the players that destroyed any good he might be doing. Everyone was 'an effing c***' and 'no wonder you are down near the bottom of the table' ... he was literally screaming at them. And then he done the worst thing any coach can do: he joined in the practice game. They was a man short and instead of taking out another man to practise what he wanted he took the empty spot. It's a cardinal sin for a coach at this level.

So the practice begins and a young lad on the right side – Maslan, I think – decided to pass the ball square to Worden instead of pushing it forward. The ball is intercepted and the opposition team went through to score. The verbal tirade Worden rained on this young lad was absolutely disgusting and even worse than the usual rants to the squad.

That was it for Maslan and he started to come across the pitch towards Worden. Thankfully a couple of the other players came and blocked his way.

When the session ended, I went over to Worden. I told him he was lucky to be on the other side of the pitch and that people were there to stop Maslan from smashing his face in. 'The square ball might have been a mistake but you do not have the right to speak to anybody like you did,' I added. 'Keep doing that and you will lose the wheels to your car. All respect will be out the window.'

'Aaah,' Worden said with a dismissive wave of his hand. 'This is football. You know what it's like.'

'Yes, I do,' I retorted, 'and that's not how it is done. The football I have learnt while here in Malaysia is very different to how it is back home. You might get away with the verbal rantings in England but not here.'

I reported back to Datuk Anifah, who just nodded and said it was 'up to me now'. I don't know what he said but I went to the next home game a couple of weeks later and there was a different Worden on the touchline. I had gone along on the Friday and was at the final training and actually heard him say 'Bad luck,' something I never thought I would hear from him when a player had made a mistake. Worden had been a successful coach but it was how he handled the success that maybe was a failing. Just under a year and he was gone from Sabah.

Sometimes I do blame the coaches as well for the short-term nature of their control. It seems that once they have a job they are looking for the next one and that means that the clubs lose any chance of stability. I always refer back to Alan Vest in Sarawak but he is the prime example. Give someone the time and resource and they can build a club!

As you can imagine, I was back at the academy and enjoying that when news of Worden's departure was confirmed and, obviously, it was not long before Datuk Anifah was on the phone.

# AN OLD FRIEND ARRIVES

'KEN, JUST do the state job for a couple of weeks while we try to find a replacement,' said Datuk Anifah. I agreed, but Datuk was crafty and as the two weeks was coming to an end, he said, 'Do you reckon we can get a good English player?'

I offered to make a few phone calls to some old agents I still had contact with. It wasn't long before David Rocastle was on his way over.

Now David was a smashing guy: a good player, a hard worker and a genuinely nice man. But I suppose they conned me a bit on the state side of things as they wouldn't let me leave the post immediately and I had to keep with the first team for a while. I loved to coach but my desire was to be with those kids I had worked so hard with to develop their skills. My assistant Azah was good but he needed the help, and I didn't know anyone else of Azah's ability to come and help him out.

This was the beginning of the end for the academy and worst of all, the man behind it all, Datuk Anifah, had moved into politics and so was obliged to step down from any involvement in state football, including the academy. We had no support, so everything was a fight from then on.

I wish I knew what happened to the boys after the academy closed.

I was still there working with David but even then there were times when we really didn't know what the hell was going on at the top. There was one game where David was playing and none of the team would pass the ball to him. To this day we don't know why but I have a feeling the game was fixed and that the players had been told keep the ball away from David. They knew he wouldn't put up with it and quite rightly at half-time he came up to me and said, 'Ken, they won't give me the effing ball. I ain't going out for the second half.' He didn't, and we lost.

On another occasion I remember the opposition keeper kicking the ball out and it bounced in the centre circle. David chested it and volleyed it straight back over the keeper's head into the goal. Even Raja Ahmad who was watching made an amusing comment: 'That isn't Rocastle, that's rascal!'

I really enjoyed working with David, though. We were two peas in a pod when it came to attitude and devotion to our work. He was with his family here and his two kids went to a local school. He was part of the community and he would always come down to the field and join in the training with the academy boys when he had time. I am not sure who enjoyed it most, David or the boys, but knowing David, it was done for the right reasons – because he wanted to! It was another very sad day when David passed away and I will never forget that for the tribute game at Arsenal, David's son was their mascot.

# THE NEXT
# CHAPTER UNFOLDS

SABAH DOES hold another not-so-fond memory and that
was when I brought my then-wife, Pat, out to visit. I knew what
I wanted her there for and this was mainly that I didn't want
things to end with a phone call or a letter. I felt that face to face
was the only way. I remember hearing her swear for the first
time: 'What the effing hell have you brought me to Sabah for?'

What I hadn't realised though was that the timing of my
decision to end it all face to face was on 4 July, our wedding
anniversary. It was something that had been on my mind for
a long while now and it had to happen, as sad as it always is,
it had to be this way. This played a big part in my relationship
with Jeany. We were friends and had remained so over the time
I was in Sabah. I had told her from the start that we would
only be friends while I was married and that I would be getting
a divorce. I am a lucky man. Jeany waited and was patient
and stood by me through a lot of troubling times when I was
making that decision to end my marriage. I thank her for that.

As divorces go, it was very smooth. Pat got the house, she
paid the legal fees and before I knew it the decree nisi was
through and the door was open for me and Jeany to tie the
knot. I don't think I actually proposed to Jeany. They have a

different way of doing things and basically it was like a family meeting where the family signed a bit of paper saying they were happy for us to get married. That 'meeting' was about 45 minutes long and I don't think I knew more than a handful, but they were deciding my fate!

Jeany and I got married in December 2000. The wedding itself was a very low-key affair. Neither of us wanted the pomp and ceremony; we knew we wanted to be together so, really, what more did we need? We had the formalities to go through, of course, which included having our photos on display in the registrar offices in Donggongon, Penampang, just in case someone didn't like the fact that we were getting married (I think the correct term was 'objections'). They was on display for two weeks, after which time we got the all clear.

With Jeany's brother Joe and his wife Elizabeth as our witnesses, we walked out as man and wife. That was also the time when we started to build our wooden house on the land Jeany had been given.

My time in Sabah was coming to an end but the whole face of football in Malaysia was changing as well. Once the ruling about politicians being involved in the game came into force, a lot of clubs lost their source of support for funding and suchlike. The main problem being that the decision seemed to be made so quickly; one day it was announced and within a couple of weeks it was enforced. If the clubs had the time to prepare a contingency plan, then maybe things would have been better. It was the correct thing to do as politics and sport do not have the greatest of relationships worldwide but it still could have been handled in a far more proactive way. They were dark days for Malaysian football and something that they have taken a long, long time to recover from. You could even say they are not at the level they should have been in today's game. There is now a light at the end of the tunnel and I am just pleased we are now away from that long dark road of before.

I was proud, though, of my achievements at the academy as quite a lot of the boys who came through my ranks went into the first team for the state. I couldn't ask for any more!

# WHAT A GREAT BUNCH

I THEN got a call from MIFA, the Malaysian Indian Football Association, asking me to head up their academy and to come to Kuala Lumpur to discuss the job. In KL, I had a long chat with T. Mohan and S. Pathy, the prime movers and shakers in MIFA. It was only a weekend gig and the money was good. I got offered a good flat and moved back to KL.

Best of all, my wife now, Jeany, was coming with me. I was a very happy man.

It was around that time that Scott O'Donnell, an old player of mine who I had brought over from Australia to play for KL, called me up and asked whether I would be interested in some part-time work during the week. He was now working for the AFC as their technical director. The deal was I would be a technical analyst. Monday to Friday I would watch, study a number of games a week, report on them and get paid a fee for every three games. That was how I got into the AFC and it worked pretty well.

I also had the pleasure of working with Bojan Hodak, a Croatian footballer and coach who Scott had also brought in to work at the AFC.

Both being footballers, we hit it off straight away and I remember many a good laugh with him.

I remember his son, Luka, who was about two years old at the time when he came to one of my training sessions. Now in all my footballing days no one ever got the better of me by passing the ball through my legs, but little Luka had a ball at his feet, so I asked him to kick the ball through my legs.

That he did but he also went through at the same time. Most definitely a first and I haven't laughed so hard again on the training ground. And I am pleased to say he is following in his dad's footsteps and becoming a good little footballer. I wish him well. And Bojan is currently head coach of the Malaysian national U-19 team.

Anything football-wise that Asian clubs were involved in, I would be watching, from the Asian Champions League, AFC Cup games and Asian World Cup qualifiers to the Asian Cup. Analyse those teams involved, the players as well, and write a report. These reports would be used when they come to select players of the season for AFC. They knew they could pass the buck on to me when someone asked who was selected for the award!

My job at MIFA was to set up football schools in Selangor to start with, and if all was okay there we could open up in other states. It was a position I enjoyed because no one interfered; I was given a job to do and I could get on with it. I was training the young lads and honestly they were the most respectful, most polite kids I have ever worked with and probably ever will. There were two-hour sessions every Saturday and Sunday and boy, did they want to learn. To start with, I covered three centres on each day and yes, there was a lot of driving, but they provided a car for me.

MIFA also appointed their coaches so they were learning from me at the same time. What I liked about their coaches was that when I was doing a practice they were always asking what and the why. I would always arrive early, as did they, and we would sit and talk through the work we would do that day. I remember one of the coaches, at the Puchong School, I think. He had a very loud voice. Not aggressive or nasty, just naturally loud! I noticed the younger kids backing off though as they thought he was angry! So I had to move him to an older group who were less likely to get upset.

I think by the end of it we had around 16 schools in Selangor and despite the travelling it was a good time in my footballing life. I just wish there could have been an end product for them, like a professional team, to progress to but in my time there we had not got to that stage. I will always wish them well, especially Mohan and Pathy. They put their money where their mouths were and all the boys who trained with us should be thankful to them. As it stands now Mohan has progressed with MIFA and all the hard the work put in by everyone has brought its rewards. The team have progressed so well, they are now in the same league as Sabah and they have been crowned Malaysian champions.

A fantastic achievement, a great reward and long may it continue.

There was a tournament in Italy and a MIFA team had gone over as a curtain raiser to their introduction the year before. Not such a good tournament for them as the best result they got was losing 12-0! Anyway, I was asked to go around Peninsular Malaysia and pick the best U-18 team I could find as they were planning to send a team again. I had my team of coaches to look after the kids and off I went.

Now, there were a lot of good players, but they were individual players and how they might work in a team was anybody's guess.

We selected our squad of players and brought them together to work for a couple of weeks before we went to Italy. They were a good group of guys and the biggest defeat was 4-0 and we saved our best until last. The media from Malaysia were there and it was so funny as they had camped out by our goal, expecting the opposition to be scoring. We scored first and it was so funny to watch the photographers scrambling to get to the other end of the field. I was sitting on the bench and the goal went in and we were all up on our feet and running on to the pitch. It did make me laugh and I will never forget that. The final score was 2-2.

After the tournament on our way to the airport, we stopped off for a while to visit the Vatican before flying home.

I am not a highly religious person, but I have to say it is an awesome experience and it did have an effect on me. I just stood, mouth open and looked around; it was one of the most spectacular things I have ever witnessed.

We had achieved something which was so special for the team. Those lads did us all proud, both on and off the pitch! MIFA was a great time for me and it is good to see them still doing well in the local leagues. I was very grateful to be there at the start.

It was shortly after that, the AFC asked me to go full-time.

I remember discussing it with Jeany and we decided we would do it for two years. This was when I came across a Japanese player playing for Gamba Osaka. Yasuhito Endo was a midfield player and the greatest honour I can pay him is he was a Japanese version of Alan Hudson. In one of the games I covered, he made 83 passes and only three went astray. This was Alan; what I used to say was 'He lends you the ball but is always around to get it back if needed.' There was no box to box, chasing up and down like a blue-arsed fly but just a conductor of the orchestra. At the time of writing he was still playing in Japan and I wish him all the best in his footballing career.

There was another chap called Mohan Thambirajah in KL and he and I set up the Chelsea Supporters' Club in KL just before I moved back to Sabah. It is still operational, I believe, and all down to his hard work. There are times when I would like people to appreciate the hard work being put in by people who just have a great love of our great team, all for no financial gain. We must never forget that without our supporters the game would be without any atmosphere and I feel the clubs should help them more financially. It doesn't have to be large amounts but just enough to keep them going.

It was also around this time that I asked Nick Atkinson to help me write my biography. We were sitting in Sid's Pub, Damansara Heights, with the usual pint of Kilkenny and the idea took shape. The result is in your hands now and I must thank Geoff Siddle for all his support with delicious pints of Kilkenny always on tap each time we finished a section of the book. Maybe that's why it took me so long!

# HOME IS MOST DEFINITELY
# WHERE THE HEART IS

THIS WAS when I started to realise how much of a home Sabah had become and that I really wanted to go back.

It was strange as well in that there were things going on at MIFA that had changed, and I felt that I was not really needed anymore.

There was a short period when we went back to Sabah but the work that I did for AFC was soon to become full-time, and so it was back to KL and a lovely flat in Bukit Jalil.

They were a great group of people to work with at AFC.

It was one of the places where you always wanted to be in early. A lot of laughter and a great environment. They actually gave everyone a suit and a tie and left the choice of shirt colour to us: blue or white!

I mentioned above about how Sabah was what I now called home, wherever I was living. This was because of Jeany's kampung, Minintod, and a piece of land on a hill. I remember the day they took me up to see it. There was no road all the way up and it was about the size of a football pitch. I was told it was ours for nothing but there were a few rules and regulations, the main one being that you had to start the foundations of a house within three months. We put a fence around it and we used to go up every now and again to do bits and pieces.

The area needed to be cleared, though, and within a day of asking the bulldozer was up there to clear the undergrowth. Then it was the water tanks to collect the rainfall for the house. It still works to this day, except when it doesn't rain! We designed the house ourselves and it was definitely a team effort with other people of the village always there to help out. There were laughs as well, like when one of the workers fell into the tub of cement we were making as a foundation for the tower for the water tanks. Almost up to his waist, he was, and when we pulled him out this boots were still there. They still are to this day!

We provided the food and drinks and, after 4pm, the beer! It was such a fantastic way to build a home and we lived there until we built our bungalow on the same plot.

Can you imagine, no electricity to drill through huge concrete pillars? We had to do it all with gut-busters. When everybody comes to help, it is called gotong-royong in Sabah and we now have a most beautiful home.

I am not sure exactly what it was that made us do the final move back to Sabah but I think it was a weekend we spent there with Jeany's family and actually thought about her family and how her parents were not getting any younger and almost decided there and then that Sabah was gonna be the home base. Jeany needed to be there with her father especially. The road wasn't finished, there was no air conditioning, it was hot and sweaty at night, and the mosquitos were ever present. But I was like a kid in a toy store and the pride in building your own home is indescribable.

Our brick house was the next order of things. We knew we wanted space for Jeany's folks to stay and the wooden house would not be enough. I always remember Jeany insisting on huge foundations because we were on a hill.

Anyway, the pilings every ten metres or whatever they were called were huge, 6'x6', and they went down about six feet as well. Definitely secure and nothing has moved to this day!

That was where I found my 'diamonds'. They could have been glass, but it was one of the holes I was digging where I discovered them and I have not had the nerve to have them checked out, just in case they really were glass!

So, the foundations were down, and it was time for the walls to go up. I remember waking up one morning and looking out and the bricks on my left side were fine, coming on lovely, and then I went across to the other side and the bricks were all over the place. What the heck was going on? When I was told that pile were gonna be screed, I was all 'No, they bleedin' ain't! I bought them good bricks for a reason and that is not to cover them up!' They had to knock 'em all down and redo it and they were none too happy about that. But this was my home and it was gonna be perfect for me. Credit to the builders though, in that they did a great job overall. The whole house was very open plan and the only doors were on the bedrooms and toilets! The air circulates well and I love it!

When I wanted to get some tiling done by the kitchen, my regular builder admitted he weren't that handy with tiling and he could recommend someone. The chap comes up, has a look and says he could but he couldn't start for a month. I spoke to my builder and confirmed the measurements and the price per square foot. Everything was agreed on, but when the guy came and did the job, guess what, he had a different figure! I didn't want to pay but then my guy took me to one side, apologised and explained that he hadn't realised but the tiler was what you might call a 'rough one' and that it may be safer to pay up and get on with it. It was not that much more than quoted, so I paid. Thankfully, a good job had been done so I was okay with things.

We finally had a brick home with electricity!

Here in this house that would be called Chelsea Hill, we were most definitely at home with nature and we even had a couple of doves. They lived very happily in their coop and they were always there with us and would even eat out of our hands. One day, when we came back from town, one of them was fairly frantic by the driveway as we arrived. Not sure what was going on, we walked across and saw that the other one had ended up in the pond and was flapping away in an attempt to get out. Jeany was straight in there and rescued it. We took it inside and Jeany dried it with the hairdryer, crushed up a Panadol and fed it to the dove with a matchstick. It survived. When we had the forest fire that was rapidly approaching their coop, it was Jeany who went and removed them as they were too scared to get out.

One of the doves used to follow me everywhere and he would walk behind me just like a dog would do. Another pet we had was a monkey and I got on well with him but if Jeany came near me he would chase her away and believe me, they can bite.

One of the proudest moments of my life was when our daughter Kenya arrived. She is now six years old and is an endless bundle of joy to me. Watching her take her first steps, say her first words and watching her grow daily makes me so proud. She speaks English, Malay, the local Kadazan dialect, and a smattering of Chinese for good measure. She obviously has Daddy wrapped around her little finger, but I know that Jeany is there to keep her in line. Every day it is worth getting up just to see them both and I know that Kenya will be my princess forever. It's a very non-materialistic existence where we live, and I think this is possibly the best environment for Kenya as she grows up. My Chelsea Hill is complete with Jeany and Kenya by my side.

# CHELSEA WITH ME
# ONCE AGAIN ...
# BUT JUST IN NAME

I SET up my Chelsea Soccer School once I was back in Sabah with excellent help from Adrian New, who was Chelsea director for Asia, to give the local kids a chance to learn about the game that I love. Not only that but also to learn about teamwork and respect. Every weekend there are a great bunch of kids who come along, pay a small fee and get the coaching that they all need. I would love to make it free but sponsorship is hard to come by and sadly even Chelsea doesn't help out. Adidas has been very helpful with regard to supplying footballs but without finances, keeping the school going could be difficult.

Adrian had done a great job with the soccer schools but since he left it is just a drifting ship with little hope for the young players we have. Most of them are under 13 years old and we do have a few younger kids. We work, as I have always done, to help them with what they are good at. I believe their weaknesses will improve with time and they will strive to make sure they understand the right technique to be able to practise on their own.

My coaches are all ex-state players and players I had when I was their coach. It is great to see they are now putting something back into the game that gave them a good career.

My right-hand man Azah Ezrein has been a vital part of me ever since I came to Sabah and I must say how lucky I have been to have such good people working with me all my time in Malaysia: Azah here in Sabah and Azlan and Ismail in KL.

The bush fires have been the only frightening occurrence while we have been there, and we are just grateful that nothing has been damaged. The saddest thing is that the fires have scared off the animals. I hope it won't be too long before they return.

It is a way of life that makes me very happy and also reminds me of the early days back in East Ham growing up.

We were in KL one evening and just after midnight Jeany's phone rang. She spoke in Malay and then put the phone down. She then called her mum back in Sabah, speaking in the local dialect. I obviously didn't have a clue what was being said. She finished the call with her mum and then made another call, in Malay again, and finally put the phone down. She explained that the friends from down the hill wanted to drink some beer from the shop.

And the best part and what really reminded me of growing up was that Jeany's mum got the beer out, got the money off the guys, threw them the keys and asked them to lock up after and chuck the keys back over the fence! I am smiling even now and wonder where we have gone wrong as it is just not possible to live that way anymore ... except where I call home!

The shop is something that we had provided for a while now for the locals. It supplied just bits and bobs for daily use in the kampung. We had the four-wheel drive, so it was easier to get to the wholesaler, load up the boot, bring it back and stack our shelves. We actually ended up being more like a pub as the locals would come up, have their beer, watch the TV we had up there and at weekends after the football even do a bit of karaoke.

Up Chelsea Hill we did not disturb no one else!

On the last Thursday of the month there is a group who used to go walking up the hills who asked if they could bring their own food and cook it at the shop. So, that Thursday became a feast. All we had to do was supply the gas for the gas rings at the back of the shop. It was always a good night and usually ended up with karaoke! Gradually, more and more people used to come, so it became a late night for us but that was no problem as we were already at home. This is typical of Sabahans and one of the many reasons I love this place.

# A FEW MORE WORDS

THE LAST 60,000 or so words have highlighted the joy I got from the beautiful game and how my passion for football gave me a great life. That said, I have to say a few more words on what I feel has worked to the detriment of the game in modern times. Some things you may agree with, others maybe not, but these are the thoughts and concerns of someone with over 60 years in football and I think I can honestly say I have seen it all!

**The Game** In the beautiful game of football, if you don't enjoy it and have a bit of fun, it is dead as a dodo. This was a key piece of the game that I grew into back in the day and I do wonder where it is now. I can't remember who said it first to me, maybe it was Tommy, but anyway I was told 'the fans need us as much as we need them!' This possibly comes back to the loyalty issue and how loyalty in my day was earned.

It wasn't a God-given right and bloody hell, did you work hard for it. We had great camaraderie with the fans back at Chelsea as we were able at that time to walk down the street with them, have a beer with them and a bit of friendly banter would always be exchanged.

And I always remember how it used to be running out of the tunnel and hoofing the ball as I got to the touchline and running on to the pitch to the ecstatic roar of the crowd. We would then kick the ball around for a couple of minutes, go to the centre circle, toss the coin, sort out the ends and the whistle went while the crowd was still cheering. There was nothing like it! Except that time when as the captain I had run on, kicked the ball and then wondered why the cheers had turned to laughter. Turned out Terry had kept all the players back, so there I was all on my tod in the middle of the pitch.

Anyway, look at it now: the players come out for a warm-up and then back down into the changing rooms for a while, then two lines of players walking on, each with a mascot for the game and by the time the handshakes and all that fluff is done with, the whistle goes. Think about it a minute, let's say ten passes in your own half and then back to the keeper who kicks it upfield and the opposition get it. Not the best way to keep the crowd cheering and any momentum created in the crowd dissolves in a chorus of whistles. Why not hold the ball for a moment while your players move forward and then hoof it up to the opponent's box; at least that is attacking play.

And boy, would the fans love it!

I don't know a way around it and I know that it is all about strategies now, or is it just the price of sponsors and suchlike that place a greater demand on the main resource of the club, the players? I wonder if we asked the stars of today, what would they prefer?

I have been asked, 'Do they play for the weekly wages or do they play for the fans?' Those two are fairly tightly linked as one probably wouldn't happen without the other.

It is very difficult to cheer something that is negative, and we will always naturally cheer and get excited over positive action. I compare it with boxing. Just imagine the crowd if both fighters just moved around and never threw a punch – not much to cheer about!

I actually put it down to the fact that we don't play 'English' football anymore. What is that? Simply, it's 'going forward'! We won the World Cup going forward and then we changed and thought we could play like the Brazilians, for example, and we can't. We are not built to play like that and so now what do we do apart from bring in the loose-limbed foreign players and our style of play gets ever further from the 'English' football I played?

We won't win the World Cup again as all the players we play with in the EPL will be playing against us! We are actually preparing every country in the world to play against us.

Our success in tournaments has been dire for so long now and we are still trying to play a style of football that we are not capable of playing. It grates on me how we go nowhere in all these matches.

How we change it, I have no idea as it has gone too far down the road and you can't just change a squad, or can you? I actually believe Gareth Southgate can make a difference and I hope the powers that be give him a chance.

Let me say a few words on the fans. Most of them are your ordinary folk who just love the game of football and support their team, rain or shine, passing down through the generations. Then there are the thugs, who believe they have a passion for the game. I remember when I played and I might be doing a throw-in or something and the banter that would go on was brilliant. I never forget just after I got married I was playing at West Ham and in the second half I was playing over by the Chicken Run in front of the home support and the comments were flying around like 'We've all been with her', 'Does she fart in bed?' and other silly remarks but all designed to put you off a bit, make you smile, make you laugh. And at the end you get a 'Good luck, Ken, no hard feelings! Just doing our bit for the lads!' Nowadays you don't need a microphone to know what the fans are saying when the opposition gets close, and the venom in how they speak and the gesticulations. I am absolutely horrified that it has come to this. There are also the objects thrown at players, referees and linesmen. The 2018 FIFA World Cup was a horrible example of how low the game can get! And I am sorry to say that it becomes more and more difficult to separate the good from the bad and the ugly.

**The Squad** It just gets bigger and bigger, doesn't it? Look at Chelsea now with the number of players in the squad. Managers manage but for the players it is vital that they keep playing.

So, does a bigger squad make things better?

I don't know the exact number but at Chelsea there are around 40 young players who are on loan to other clubs. Are they originally signed just to get them off the market? Now, yes, in most cases the club loaning the players covers their wages but there will always be the case where a club cannot afford the full whack, so Chelsea make up the shortfall.

Anyone with any football knowledge though will know that if you want to better your game you play with better players. If someone is on loan it is most probable that the team is of a lower standard than Chelsea. The top clubs all have their big squads as well, so they don't want the loan players.

So I am not sure how this strategy works to the benefit of the club. I honestly just don't get it. Money may not be a problem but is it really making a difference to the game as a whole? If you are gonna invest in a player and not actually play them, what is the point? Are they being signed so that no one else can sign them?

The loan situation, I understand, is now a topic of conversation among football's governing bodies and about bloody time too!

**Substitutes** I can't move on without a word or two about substitutes! A bugbear that really frustrates me in the modern game. How many bloody substitutes do you need?

You read before what I said about how it was when I started playing. The one substitute you had was only used if a player was injured. Okay, that was abused, like the time we was playing at Spurs and Tommy calls me over to the bench and says, 'Tell Mike to pull a muscle.' This I did and Mike was quite theatrical with his feigned injury. Oscars all around for the performance and the referee smiled, he knew it was maybe not the best of rules, but still the stretcher came on and off went Mike to the cheers and laughter of both sets of supporters.

I am not against substitutions. Don't get me wrong, but come on: seven players on the bench and three subs! Keep it to three: one goalie and two outfields. I also detest it when the game is in the closing minutes and the leading team or whatever decides to make a change to waste time. To be honest with you it is strategically a crazy move because if the player is not injured or anything, you are disrupting the flow of the game and any continuity you may have is gone, and we have seen it pay the ultimate price of a goal against the run of play!

And for those players on the bench who don't even get the chance to play in the reserves for fear of injury, I know how easy it is to get 'rusty'. So you can imagine the scene where the player hasn't played for six weeks and then it is 'Okay. On you go!' and the player is expected to have all his timing and judgement correct. Fat chance! I remember talking to a Chelsea player a few years ago and he was a regular on the bench and had hardly had a full competitive match, so his touch and fitness were lower than the regular players. In one match, he was told to warm up to go on for the last 30 minutes. His touch was not there, his timing was poor and the fans turned against him. What chance did he have after not playing a competitive game for months? I think all substitutes should play regular reserve team football to retain their touch and fitness.

As I write these words, we have a classic example in a recent Chelsea game. John Terry hasn't played for a number of weeks, then comes on the pitch, his timing is out and he mistimes a tackle, straight red card! Was this his fault or the system's?

This is even more important for the goalkeeper, as his timing and his reactions can more likely decide the outcome of a game. It is most definitely a very different game from training and the keeper is potentially more in the crosshairs of blame when a goal goes in.

The other thing with the goalkeeper is the communication with the team-mates in front of him, particularly the defenders. This is vital to the efficiency of a team. Remember, he can see everything and the information he passes to his defenders is of great importance and creates the basis of a solid team. When I see teams training and the goalkeepers are doing their own thing, I feel this is time wasted as the opportunity to create a bond between the goalkeeper and his defenders is crucial. Ask any defender and he will tell you the importance of a vocal goalkeeper.

There also seems to be this constant friction of club and country. When I played, the pinnacle of your career was to play for your country. Okay, money has come into the game and it is the clubs who pay the wages but come on, where has the pride gone? But that is not the worst thing in my mind. When a player says he is retiring from international football, 'Bullshit,' I say. They are more concerned that they might not get picked again. The likes of Bobby Charlton and Bobby Moore would never have dreamed of quitting the national team.

**The Referee** I have always said that the respect shown to a referee in a rugby game is far and away so much greater than that shown to a football referee by the players. In my day, there was a different type of professionalism. It was a hard game and more often than not the only time you stayed on the ground after a tackle was if you physically couldn't get up.

I'm not saying we was perfect 'cos there were a number of hard men in the game but it was still fair. None of this rolling around as if you have been mortally wounded and screaming at the ref to give a card to the tackler. That is actually one of my least favourite parts of today's game.

You know who I mean, and it really pains me to see these so-called professionals trying to get another player sent off. They should be carded immediately if they make any comment to the ref. Some rules have now come into force whereby people can't hassle the ref so much, but it still goes on and combined with the play-acting it makes the ref's job doubly difficult.

Let me go back to rugby. There is so much we can learn from it. The video referee comes into play quite often and there are rules for a restart. I wonder sometimes how we might do a restart in football but we seem to cope when there is a head injury and play has to be held up. I think too many people make too many excuses as to why this and why that and it amazes me that with the money involved nowadays there is not more video, used to sort out decisions.

But it is good to see that this is changing as I write this down.

Don't get me started on the acting that goes on. If someone has dived or over-exaggerated, check the video and put them in a sin bin for ten minutes. Disrupt their team!

Then at the opposite end of the scale and you get the bully, who just uses intimidation to get his way. I think the person who said that if half of the people playing in the Premier League weren't playing football they would be in prison got it right!

We see quite often now that a manager gets sent to the stands. Is that how to lead a team? I look to the FA and would like to ask how many on the panels have actually experienced football, someone who knows the off- and onfield tactics and shenanigans?

The referee cannot see everything and even with two linesmen and a fourth official things will be missed. There needs to be more respect and as my dad once said, 'That's why the referee is in black, he's the policeman!' I pray that the authorities get their act together!

My all-time favourite was Jim Finney, the best referee by a mile. I will never forget his words when I came out as captain for Chelsea at home against Sunderland. Me and the Sunderland captain joined him in the centre circle to flip the coin and he said, 'Have a good game lads and let's hope I don't make as many mistakes as you!' Great words from a great man.

**Corruption** This will always be something that, sadly, stains the good name of football. Maybe it could be said of any sport, especially where gambling is involved. And this is where it becomes a joke because it isn't gambling any more if the result is fixed.

We recently heard on the news that Malaysia is recognised as allegedly the worst place for match-fixing in the region. I must be honest and say, yes, I have witnessed this, but it is a worldwide problem and when you see what has happened at FIFA in recent times, is it any surprise? I remember hearing someone say once that the reason FIFA were so against video referees is that it could go against any match-fixing, in effect giving the chance for a review!

Whatever their reason, nothing would surprise me anymore. My beautiful game has changed.

In my younger days, I always remember the pools: Littlewood's and Vernon's. What was it now? Score draws, no score draws and 'lucky 6'. Was there match-fixing then?

This is something that needs to be addressed from the top down and I suppose what worries me is that it is now so entrenched in every element that we may never have a clean sport for all to enjoy. I honestly pray for the day.

Saddest of all was when my old friend Sam Allardyce was allegedly caught raiding the cookie jar. A very sad moment for me as I know the guy and that was never a part of his character. Times change, I know, and maybe it is those people who surround you at these times who are also to blame. I know Sam would not have organised this, so I should ask why it is seemingly just him who gets the bullet and not also the agent who brought it all to bear?

And that leads nicely on to my next frustration.

**The Agent** In my playing days, you had an agent. He was the guy who sorted your insurance for your car and the road tax, helped with getting your mortgage, checked you paid your taxes, and kept you on the straight and narrow legally and had no dealings whatsoever with the management on your contract.

Oh, how it has changed.

The agents have sneaked into the game and seemingly rule the roost. Half the time I don't know whether the players have any idea about who the agent is talking to and money rears its ugly head again. I am not against people making money but, come on, it has to be done with a bit of dignity, a bit of class.

The great Brian Clough summed it up perfectly when he said, 'I don't want to talk to any agent. I want to talk to that guy who is asking for 200 quid a week and I am only offering 100. If he really fights me for what he believes he is worth, then that is my player. If he comes back with, "Okay, then I will take 100," I don't want him!'

I know it is a cut-throat and complicated world out there but they should man up and not rely on agents who are more concerned with their percentage. Look at what happened recently with one player whose agent has gone to the press about his player not being played enough and complained that a birthday cake wasn't given on the player's birthday, among other moans. Excuse me but we are talking about adults here. We are not in nursery school anymore.

We all have our place and I am sorry to say but the agents, not all I must say, but too many, have overstepped their mark and I hope that the regulatory bodies also grow a pair and stamp this out before it rules the game more than it already does.

**Fitness** I must say something on fitness as it seems to be a common excuse among the playing elite of today. All too often we hear about fixture congestion and too many games. When I was at the top of my game we had 42 league games, plus the FA Cup, the League Cup, the InterCity's Fairs Cup and that was before the internationals! The rule with international games was that if one member of your squad was selected, your regular games went ahead. If two or more were selected the relevant league game could be postponed. So, as far as the number of games goes, not that different. So, I do ask sometimes, why are they so tired? I am sick to death of hearing that excuse. If I had said that to Tommy Docherty, for example, he would have said I needed more training as I wasn't fit enough!

And the other thing is that it is only a relatively small number who continually complain. Is it not the same for everyone?

When we played, if there was a knock or a strain, we had a 'man with a sponge'. Don't get me wrong, that was probably not the best way to treat it but nowadays there is a whole team of physiotherapists, specialists, dieticians, etc.

I can just imagine Terry Venables having to eat what he was told. You get what I mean, though. No pie and mash and no trip on Saturday evening to Barny's in Aldgate!

Is all this pandering good for the game?

And then this rotation thing. In my day if the team had played well and you were all fit, it would be the same team the following week.

That is the game of today though and I still say that if you are paid a crazy wage to play for the club, then you make sure you are fit enough. Injury, fair enough.

But tiredness? No way!

**Foreign Players** I am not against foreign players, but I am against the number of foreign players. Some games I watch there are as many as 14 to 16 foreign players on the field. Our young English players have just won the FIFA U-17 World Cup and I wonder how many will be playing in the EPL next season. I know clubs are under pressure for success, but you only have to look and you will see that most of the successful teams in the EPL are owned by foreign people and their objective is success. Okay, I understand and accept that, but I am not so sure it is good for our national team.

# SITTING ON TOP OF
# MY CHELSEA HILL

LOOKING BACK, I have had plenty of ups and downs in my career. After having a very promising playing career ruined by injury, I then had ten years with Chelsea as youth manager and coach and two years as team manager, then various other managerial opportunities where I was always with people I sincerely respected. I always wanted to play football but there comes a time when you have to be realistic and turn your life to something else. It was Chelsea who gave me the chance to be in charge of their original development programme, an opportunity that was very good for me but also changed the direction of my skills from the playing to the coaching.

To work with young highly talented players was the perfect compensation for having to retire early from playing.

I have said before that as a youth coach the job is to identify talented players and work with them without being a bully.

This we done and the young players responded tremendously well and I have great respect for what the young players have gone on to achieve. They will always be a fantastic part of my life that I will never forget, and it makes me especially proud to see those that have gone on to become highly successful players, managers, coaches and, most of all, good people.

I do still wonder as I sit here at my home on Chelsea Hill, what is the future of football? It is commonplace now for some story to appear in the press, whether about corruption, match-fixing or the latest scandal about one of the so-called role models we have as players now. Week in and week out I see disgusting tackles that can end a player's career; we have to put up with the divers, cheats and players who have been fouled calling the referee to show a red or yellow card.

I don't call that professionalism; I have my own word for that. When the players meet before the match and shake hands, I don't call them handshakes anymore. I was brought up that when you shake someone's hand you look in their eyes. This is a sign of respect and even the officials, referee and linesman have been dragged down to just slapping a hand and that just says to me that very little respect exists between both parties.

Every part of the game has to come together to fix the broken parts, but the money still pours in and I shake my head. Just recently we have had the English FA show their true colours and how they just don't want to change or evolve. Who knows what will happen to the beautiful game?

Football is the greatest game in the world for me and the game most talked about ... for good and bad reasons.

All I am sure about is that it gave me more than 60 years of fun and to be honest, a bloody good life!

For me though, once again I am at the top of the Chelsea Hill and I am at home.

Thank you for listening.

# ABOUT KEN SHELLITO

KEN SHELLITO was the first and only manager of the Chelsea Football Club to have moved up through the ranks at Stamford Bridge, from ground staff to junior player to first team player to coach and finally to team manager.

He joined Chelsea at 15, turned professional in 1957 and, as a full-back, played 123 senior games for the club – as well as winning full England honours – before an injury in his left knee prematurely ended his playing career in late 1967. He coached the club's junior players after that and in December 1969 was in charge of the youth section and became the full manager of the club after 22 years with Chelsea, followed by time with Queens Park Rangers, Preston and a stint as the manager for Cambridge United.

After leaving the UK, Ken built his own footballing world in his new home of Malaysia, nurturing youth players at the football clubs of Selangor, Kuala Lumpur, Perak and, finally, Sabah.

He also established the Ken Shellito Football Academy in Penampang and was a match analyst for the Asian Football Confederation (AFC).

He spent his final years at his residence – aptly called Chelsea Hill – in Kampung Minintod, Sabah, with his wife

Jeany and their daughter Kenya. He passed away at home on 31 October 2018.

# ABOUT NICK ATKINSON

NICK ATKINSON was born and bred in the UK and didn't meet Ken until he was living and working in Malaysia. They met in 2009 over a pint of Kilkenny and Nick always says it was being in the right place at the right time that led to him being asked to help Ken with his story: 'Ken spoke, and I wrote.'

Now living in Kuala Lumpur with his wife, Nick occasionally returns to the UK but does hope to visit Stamford Bridge at some point to put a final full stop on the words he wrote for Ken. 'He was such a special guy, we laughed so much, and I am very sad that he is not here to share his story.'

Nick is sure that this will be part of Ken's legacy as he captured the attention and respect of so many in the world of football.